"Transforming a fractured team takes pr[...] made stronger through these challenging shared exercises and a deeper empathy and understanding of one another. Philip Folsom's knowledge and process were invaluable to my team building process."
-Nick Rish, Director Business Development at Apple

Your teachings inspire us to be happier and more functional humans at work and home!"
-Andy Walshe, Director of Red Bull High Performance Department

Philip Folsom has created a highly impactful and unique program. Throughout my time in the military, I've participated in many leadership programs. Team to Tribe is powerful! It has left me with a feeling of self-fulfillment, self-understanding and led us to understanding the purpose behind our personal 'why'.
-Kevin Devine, Program Manager at Space X

Philip Folsom is an incredibly effective team builder, culture creator and transition guide. The journey from Team to Tribe has made a huge impact in the professional development of so many of our students. Thanks Chief! Fight on!
-James Bogle, Director MBV Program at USC

Philip Folsom's work helped us develop our team's community and connections into a culture of health and high performance. His work with us was staggeringly impactful.
-Andy Petranek, Co-Founder of the Whole Life Challenge

"Philip Folsom's Team to Tribe is highly impactful, breaking down complex ancient life wisdom into relatable anecdotes and lessons. The Program is extremely well-organized covering some generally known concepts through an innovative approach that leaves you with a 'life roadmap' to help you not only understand yourself better but also your teammates and loved ones. I highly recommend to any individual or company wanting to gain a greater understanding of the human experience."
-Christine Romer, Red Bull Distribution Company

The next step after redesigning my team and hiring talented newcomers was to unite and focus them. Philip's Team to Tribe program was exactly what we needed. Initially drawn in as we learned about ourselves individually, we then molded together in comparison and contrast throughout each exercise – the team developed right before my eyes. Now, a few weeks later, I see increased collaboration and camaraderie daily and I know it is all because of the culture upgrade from Team to Tribe.
-Leslie Newlee, Senior Director Business Insights at Red Bull

Philip is an absolute expert of culture development, hitting on all fronts. From a micro lens, in developing teams, to a macro lens, in developing communities, Philip is truly a master of his craft. His commitment to excellence, driven by an authentic desire towards his vision of healing a sick society, is a quality far and few between!
-Corey Castillo, Ed.D

Team to Tribe

The Roadmap for reclaiming kinship
and success in your family and career

The ancient wisdom of the tribe triangle by

Philip Folsom

Copyright © 2023 by Philip Folsom

All rights reserved. No part of this book may be reproduced or used in any manner without written permission of the copyright owner except for the use of quotations in a book review.

For more information visit: www.philipfolsom.com.

First paperback edition December 2023
Cover and book design by Honter Studio

ISBN 979-8-9896374-1-6 (Hardcover)
ISBN 979-8-9896374-0-9 (Paperback)
ISBN 979-8-9896374-2-3 (eBook)

For all people living today who are reclaiming their birthright of kinship and standing on the shoulders of their ancestors.

Contents

Foreward

Preface

Introduction to the 52 Steps Up the Tribe Triangle

Phase I: Alignment

Step 1:   The Journey Toward Tribe and Why it Must Be Taken 20
Step 2:   Pride to Honor and the First Lesson of the Wolves 25
Step 3:   Alignment and Becoming the Falconer to Bring the
          Others Home 31
Step 4:   Your Shared Vision to Bring the Others Home 36
Step 5:   Values Dictate Destiny... 42
Step 6:   Shared Values Make Your People and Projects Go Far 49
Step 7:   Shared Mission, Hunting Big Game Together
          Makes Heroes 56
Step 8:   Transparency Creates Transformation 62
Step 9:   Reciprocity is the Engine of Kinship 68
Step 10: Goals Move Mission Toward Vision 75
Step 11: Your Brand is Not Logo it is Your Reputation 81
Step 12: Leadership is the Act of Creating a Future That
          Doesn't Currently Exist 87
Step 13: Change is Hard and Scary So Know Your Enemy................. 93

Phase II: Kinship

INTRODUCTION TO KINSHIP
Step 14: Reclaiming Kinship 104
Step 15: Kinship Solutions to Resiliency Challenges 109
Step 16: The Solution for Sustainable Success............................. 114

Step 17: Kindness is a Function of Kinship 119
Step 18: The Secret Power of Altruism 124
Step 19: Celebrate and Leverage the Differences in Your Tribe 129
Step 20: Upgrading from Golden Rule to Platinum Rule 133
Step 21: Who is Your Best Friend at Work? 138
Step 22: The Impact of Trust 143
Step 23: The Unexpected Power of Appreciation 148
Step 24: Mastering Communication Styles 154
Step 25: The Large-Scale Impact of Morale 161
Step 26: The Significance of Service 165

Phase III: Healthy Conflict

INTRODUCTION TO HEALTHY CONFLICT
Step 27: Healthy Conflict and the Power of Adversity 171
Step 28: The Power and Challenge of Accountability 176
Step 29: Adaptability is Applied Innovation 182
Step 30: Moving from Hunting to Killing 187
Step 31: The Power of Asking for Help and Giving It 192
Step 32: The Master Key of Commitment 197
Step 33: Claiming Competition 202
Step 34: The Power and Process of Delegation 207
Step 35: Developing Grit 214
Step 36: Emotional Intelligence and Regulation 219
Step 37: Real Respect 225
Step 38: Stretch Goals and Failure 230
Step 39: Taking Off the Armor and Coming Home 235

Phase IV: Sustainable Thriving

INTRODUCTION TO SUSTAINABLE THRIVING
Step 40: Making and Maintaining Flow State 243
Step 41: Growing Vitality 249
Step 42: Leaders Create More Leaders 255

Step 43: Self-Reflection and Growth 262
Step 44: Coaching and Standing on the Shoulders of Giants 268
Step 45: Celebrations and Traditions 274
Step 46: Growth Mindset and Preparing for War 279
Step 47: The Strength of Vulnerability 285
Step 48: The Holy Grail of Service 290
Step 49: Freedom and Meaning 295
Step 50: Becoming a Professional 301
Step 51: Recommit and Reconnect 307
Step 52: The Legacy of Reclaiming Kinship 313

The time of the lone wolf is over

In an era of disconnect, disengagement, dissatisfaction and lack of belonging a new path with ancient origins has been revealed. It is a battle-tested journey of welding the pride-based, lone wolf individuals in our families and work teams into something greater than the sum of their parts. It is the reclamation of kinship which includes:

- Setting an aspirational vision for the future that provides meaning and hope
- Crafting a set of shared values that drive powerful decision-making and commitment
- Establishing shared missions that activate collaboration and reciprocity
- Unlocking the unique potential of aligned individuals to unlock innovation and resiliency
- Building the new generations of leaders to power growth and legacy

Team to Tribe is your step-by-step roadmap to build an aligned, sustainably successful family and organization and navigate the journey of reclaiming kinship in the world. It will be the most meaningful leadership achievement of your life and the key to your legacy in the world.

Philip Folsom is an anthropologist, army veteran and author. He is recognized as an industry leader in organizational culture development and resiliency and lectures at USC where he provides leadership development classes at the Marshall School for Business.

Philip is also the president of Wolf Tribe, an international consulting agency that delivers transformational leadership and culture development programs to major organizations such as Space X, Google, Disney and Red Bull where he sits on their High-Performance Board.

Philip is the co-founder of the critically acclaimed Valor Resiliency Program for veterans, first responders, entrepreneurs and other men and women in high stress fields. He is also the co-founder of the international K4 School of Men's Work, an acknowledged leader in the field of men's leadership development.

Philip lives with his wife, daughter and Belgian Malinois in Venice Beach, California.

Foreward, Team to Tribe

I've always been more than a little jealous of people who've had those life-altering epiphanies, those moments that seem to magically morph them into better versions of themselves. Does that *really* happen? I had gone decades without mine, so I didn't believe that I'd ever have that type of transformational experience.

But then, it happened.

You see, for several years, every Saturday morning I was part of a group of over 100 people who gathered to hear world-class experts share their knowledge on every subject under the sun.

And one day, Philip came to speak.

He shared insights he uncovered from studying ancient tribal cultures, anthropology, sociology, animal behavior, and high performing teams. He drew a through-line between these disciplines in a way that touched something deep within me.

I found myself unconsciously nodding and muttering "yes, yes, yes" based on his observations about the nature of the world and how we should be living within it. His words accessed a knowing that I had vaguely felt but wasn't able to clearly articulate before hearing them expressed in his unique way.

After hearing his talk, I needed more, so I approached him and received an invitation to join an ongoing gathering at his home. Other than my wife, I had no place to explore my deeper thoughts, hopes, fears, and victories, and I was sold when I received an invitation from him that ended with "The time of the lone wolf is over."

I literally cried.

I had found my tribe.

Every week we sat around a massive firepit to discuss the history and current state of masculinity in the world. We learned new structures, shared our "shadows and gold" of the week, and created the kind of kinship that is so lacking in today's world. Our society is sick because of a lack of authentic connection and meaning, which can be cured through kinship.

Philip's work, beautifully articulated in this book, provides an antidote to that pervasive sickness.

Sometimes, it's not so much about learning something new as it is hearing things in a fresh way that moves you into action. That is Philip's gift. He is a synthesizer who has gone on the hero's journey and brought back gifts, lessons, ways to see and act in this world that can make a huge difference in the quality of one's life. As an example, his interpretation of the male archetypes of King, Warrior, Magician, and Lover was tectonic for me. It literally shifted me to higher ground as a father, husband, friend, colleague, and advisor.

In this book, you will find the gems Philip has uncovered during his deep exploration into the field of leadership development. He has worked with executive teams at companies like Red Bull, Space X, and Disney, and when I invited him to partner with me on a presentation to a major law firm, he skillfully unpacked the need for something far greater than immediate profit and production. He got them to understand that to thrive, to be fully engaged, innovative, and resilient requires a culture that encourages greater meaning and kinship. This is not something law firms usually think about, but it is something they desperately need.

This masterful book can become your step-by-step field guide for calling home your lone wolves, to bring them together as a tribe to become something far greater than the combination of their parts. It contains a workable blueprint for harvesting kinship, for accessing our human primal nature, to reap the benefits of higher performance both personally and organizationally.

Team to Tribe is a leadership book at its core. As Philip puts it; "Leaders are the head of culture before they are anything else", so applying the lessons in this book to become a true tribe leader is the greatest legacy you can give your family, your community, and your work teams. If you are a leader, this book is your roadmap to attracting, engaging, developing, and inspiring the kind of vision and value-aligned people that make communities thrive.

This is your playbook for becoming the kind of leader you want to be, and the kind of leader your people yearn to follow.

Indeed, the time of the lone wolf is over.

***

David Freeman, J.D., is a two-time best-selling author and Hall of Fame business development consultant who has worked with over 10,000 lawyers in hundreds of law firms worldwide.

Preface

This time last year my wife Tanya and I were stuck in a snowstorm up in the mountains. We started discussing the Hero's Journey and my writing goals and Tanya challenged me to write one step on the path of the Hero's Journey every week for the next year. These long-form blogs became the chapters of that book and I have used that strategy in the process of writing this book as well.

Tanya has always been my biggest champion which I appreciate. She has also always been my biggest challenger which I also appreciate but sometimes that takes longer to see. She's the one that got me photography workshops after seeing my passion with a camera and I loved that immediately. She's also the one that got me Jiu Jitsu classes after seeing me on the couch watching the UFC and my love for that challenge took a little longer.

The process of writing one chapter of my books a week works for me in the same way chunking down your big challenges will work for you. This is especially true for the daunting challenge of elevating the culture of your family or work team.

Every journey consists of steps. Large scale journeys require these steps to be in the right order because one step in the wrong direction can translate to being far off course later on the trip. Addressing big projects on a step by step basis also makes even the most daunting challenge manageable. There are no problems right now, only situations. Problems exist in the future.

Every journey needs a map and the biggest journeys need the best maps. The Tribe Triangle is the second of the three Master Maps of humanity and it outlines the universal and timeless sequence of steps we need to take to transform a collection of individual lone wolves into an aligned, engaged and resilient pack capable of sustainable success. This timeless process is called by many names across eras and industries but it remains the one way to make a championship sports team, dominant military force or company. It will work for your family as well.

Many of you who are reading this have worked with me and have already been introduced to this content. You know the power of alignment, kinship and healthy conflict. For those of you this will be a particularly good journey because even though it takes a month for a new practice and 3 months for a new lifestyle but a year to establish a new culture. 52 weeks is just perfect! This one year can change the entire direction of your organization or family. It's worth it.

I have been sharing these three Master Maps to organizations around the world for the past 10 years. I teach them at the USC Marshall School for Business and to leadership teams at fortune 500 companies that rely on their leadership and culture to stay competitive in today's tumultuous times. They will work for you as well.

I'm glad you are joining me on this epic journey of reclaiming kinship and sustainable success for your family and team. We're going to go to the deep and dark places you have avoided much of your life and we're also going to see some views from peaks you have never discovered.

This time next year we will all have explored and discovered the timeless and battle-tested techniques of transforming lone wolves into a committed, engaged and aligned pack capable of hunting and pulling down the biggest game.
We deserve it. Our people, projects and legacy demand it.

The reward for this journey is not just the sustainable success skills you get from the project, it is who you and your team become.

Blessings of Ubuntu to all your people and projects
Philip Folsom

Introduction to 52 Steps up the Tribe Triangle

We are built for tribe and kinship. It is the core human operating system installed by hundreds of thousands of years of evolution. Kinship permeates every aspect of our lives including resiliency, culture and biology. This operating system is made and maintained by feedback from the natural world and includes the things that make us feel good, safe and belong as well as the things that make us feel bad which include fear, hunger and loneliness. Kinship is an ancient, battle-tested survival system.

In our current era of too much food, climate-controlled buildings and no predation, kinship has become an optional choice for families and teams. We have gone from deeply interconnected, intimate and reciprocal packs to a vast sea of lone wolves who think they do not need a pack, have never been taught how a packs work and why they are important. This is proving to be a disaster for humanity.

Lone wolves do not thrive. Most do not even survive. Lone wolves cannot hunt big game and become scavengers. The same is true for lone humans. Without kinship, rates of clinical anxiety, depression, addiction and suicide skyrocket. Without kinship, engagement, retention, competitiveness and resiliency plummet.

If you are a leader of a family or team, reclaiming kinship and installing a fully modernized tribe system is your number one lever for the success of both yourself and your people. This book is your roadmap.

How to use this book

Information today is cheap and easy. The integration of information into useful, practical skills is becoming increasing hard. The pace and volume of the information is increasing and so are the endless distractions and competition for our time and attention. This degrades the focus which is required to actually explore, discover and integrate new skills. We are drowning in information and starving for wisdom.

There is a lot of information in this book. It is the product of 30 years of consulting with leaders and teams from companies such as Red

Bull, Disney, Space X and Google. In addition to the organizational development treasure trove here there is also a wealth of historical, psychological and applied anthropological information from my career of resiliency and coaching.

No book, program or coach is going to make you a better leader. Only you can do that. You gotta do the work. Firstly, if I was coaching *you*, Tribe Leader, I would demand you write down where these lessons apply in your family or team. The act of writing crystalizes information into practical, personal use. It makes it *useful*. The word *spelling* implies both magic and writing and it is both. There are several journal prompts at the end of each chapter for you to do this indispensable work of transforming interesting information into powerful wisdom.

You will not want to do these writing challenges at the end of each chapter and there will be the familiar resistance of *not enough time, I don't know how or I don't need to.* This is just the first adversity you will face in changing the culture of your team. If you cannot do these writing challenges, how can you hope to model these lessons and lead your team to the next level? If that sounds like a challenge from one leader to another, it is. Gauntlet thrown. You deserve the growth and transformation from that work. Your family and team demand it.

As Tribe Leader you are the Head of Culture before you are anything else. Your family and team are rarely listening to you but they are always watching. You must do the work. Fortunately, part of kinship is that we will always do more for others than we will do for ourselves. This is the essence of honor and the source of all forms of heroism in human history. We will reiterate this point many times on this journey because we need to hear this many times on this journey. Repetition is the mother of skill and studies have shown that people need to hear information at least seven times before they *actually* hear it. Be patient with yourself and your team.

Secondly, in addition to writing, Tribe Leaders must *speak*. The magical word 'abracadabra' means 'I create what I say' in Hebrew. Like writing, our words crystalize thoughts and information into actions that lead to results. There is tremendous power in them. I recommend you have a quick conversation with your family and team on each theme of these chapters. It will be the most interesting and valuable dinner conversation at home or meeting starter at work you have had in a long time. These conversations are where the magic of kinship will be cast.

All books talk. This one also listens, so talk to it. Tribe Leaders must write and speak.

A couple important notes on the term *tribe* **and the challenge of** *tribalism*

Tribe is an anthropological term denoting a small social division consisting of families or communities linked by social and economic ties and shared beliefs with a common culture and a recognized leader. We still have Tribe Culture existing in isolated pockets of our gigantic, lone-wolf world and we are obsessed with these honor-based cultures. Look at how many movies are made about the military, superhero teams, sports teams and deeply connected friend groups. These are all Tribe Cultures and we are starving for the belonging and meaning that is only found within them.

Tribe is also the most ferociously competitive culture you can create because it differentiates between those of us who are in our tribe and those who are not. This is the heart of *winning* and it exists because competition and conflict are real and eternal. If you don't see that and believe it, you should not be a leader in business or sports or maybe anything else. That competitive engine within Tribe Culture is connected to *tribalism* and it contains the tricky balance between inclusivity and exclusivity.

If you are committed to creating your team's Tribe Culture, get ready for increased competition, accountability, innovation and all the other high-octane behaviors that happen when the healthy conflict of kinship is unleashed. When you call down the thunder of tribe, get ready to ride the lightning. Here's one piece of advice about managing the challenges of tribalism while keeping the massive benefits of tribe culture itself:

Learn to love the people next to you more than you want to beat the people across from you.

*'Kindness' contains the root 'kin' and it is the special behavior
we hold for those within our tribe. We are all Tribe.*

Ubuntu is an ancient African term meaning 'I am because we are and we are because I am'. It means *humanity*. We will be repeating this word and its meaning many times on this journey because your ability to create a culture of kinship is your greatest skill as a leader. Ultimately, we are all tribe and I am truly grateful to have you with me on this epic trip up the Tribe Triangle mountain. It's an arduous journey but soon you will have a map and the view from the top is worth it.

SUSTAINABLE SUCCESS

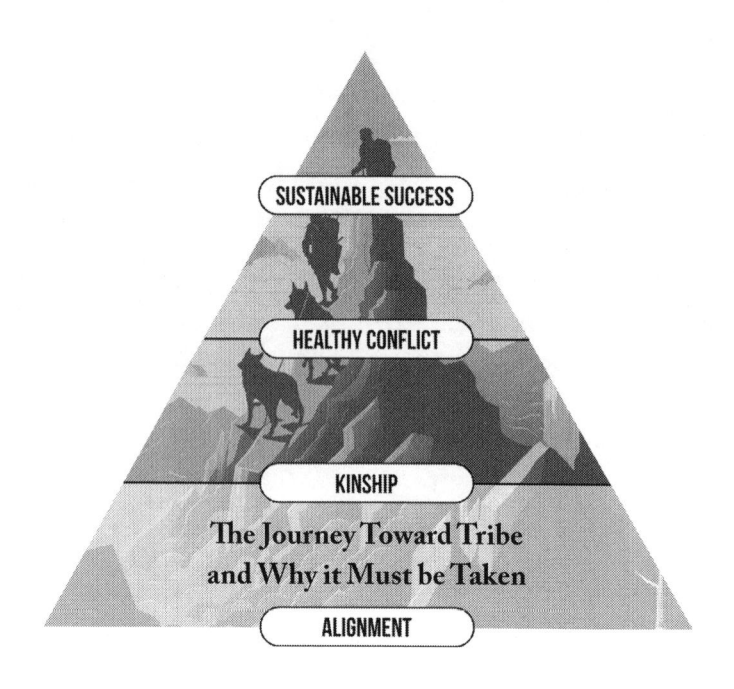

HEALTHY CONFLICT

KINSHIP

The Journey Toward Tribe
and Why it Must be Taken

ALIGNMENT

STEP 1 UP THE TRIBE TRIANGLE:

The Journey Toward Tribe and Why it Must be Taken

"The root of the word 'kindness' is 'kin'. Kinship is the heart and core of Tribe Culture and Humanity itself."

The heroic journey up the Tribe Triangle is a long and demanding quest that will force you into deep challenging introspection and development. You will face resistance from both yourself and your team. Change is hard. Growth is even harder. Before we begin this journey, I want you to know why it is so important, because if our *why* is strong enough we will figure out and endure the *how*.

In a nutshell, that *why* is the who of everyone you work with and live with. All those people are counting on you to lead and make the decisions that keep them safe and successful.

The Tribe Triangle is the ancient, time-tested sequence of steps that leaders must take to transform a group of individualistic, self-focused, lone wolves into an aligned, committed and high performing pack, family or organization. This is the only proven process to create a championship team or family that can hunt the big game of meaning and sustainable success that includes increased:

- Engagement
- Retention
- Morale
- Innovation
- Competitiveness
- Efficiency
- Resiliency

The Tribe Triangle is the way we reclaim kinship with our people and ourselves. This map exists in every truly high performing culture in the world including professional sports, elite military units and top tier leadership teams. The Tribe Triangle is the rock-solid roadmap for building an intentional, resilient and high performing *culture*.

Culture is King. It is either your family's or organization's ultimate competitive advantage and source of meaning and freedom or it is your Achilles heel. Investing in your culture has eight times the return on investment than leveling up either strategy or technology. Culture is *that* powerful because regardless of what you do in your life it will always ultimately involve *other people*. Exploring and mastering that unavoidable truth is the most valuable skill a leader can develop.

You are that leader. Leaders are head of culture before we are anything else. What leaders do literally creates culture because culture consists of the shared beliefs and behaviors of a group of people. As a leader, your position is a force multiplier of culture creation. What you model with your actions establishes the values, vision, innovation, morale and overall success of your family, work team and community. In addition, all these groups touch other groups and influence their cultures so what we do as leaders does truly echo in eternity.

Your ability to create the culture of these central groups of people in your life determines their destiny. It also dictates the happiness, morale, resiliency and quality of life on that journey towards that destiny. Culture is the way your people feel about getting together to do a project. Is it apprehension or anticipation? Insecure or innovative? Lukewarm or on fire? Transactional or reciprocal?

Ultimately, this core leadership skill of intentionally shaping culture and environment is about building *tribe*. Tribe is the ancient core operating system of our species. It is a deeply fulfilling experience of value-aligned people collaborating on significant and reciprocal projects that no individual could ever do alone. When you think of the best team you were ever on in your life it was probably in sports, the military, Greek organization or successful startup. These are all honor-based, mission-driven and value-aligned Tribe Cultures.

The Tribe Triangle is the roadmap for creating this resilient, high performing culture wherever you go. The trip up the Tribe Triangle mountain is arduous and committed but the trip and the destination are worth the work. Like all valuable things it will take *consistent work*. It takes a month to establish a new habit, three months to establish a new lifestyle and a year to grow a new culture. Hang in there, we will be doing this together and there will be incredible discoveries but you must do the writing and speaking prompts every week. Use a journal for the writing and pick your inner circle to hear your speaking. Writing and speaking are the ways we pull hidden things out of the fog so we can deal with them and make them better.

There are four stages to creating and maintaining your Tribe Culture. If you are using this book as a yearlong organizational training, we will be exploring, discovering and implementing one of these stages each quarter.

1. Creating Alignment
2. Kinship and Belonging
3. Healthy Conflict
4. Sustainable Thriving

If you are using this framework at a quicker pace, have grace with yourself and your team. Be patient and have lots of compassion on this journey of transformation.

I have divided each of these four stages of Tribe culture creation into their primary 13 steps which are the chapters in this book (one for each week of the quarter if you are using it in a year long process). For you leaders who take responsibility for the culture and success of your team or family you will see the value and be compelled to do this work. *If there is something in your team that isn't as good as it could be it is because you are not as good as you could be.* Remember, you are the Head of Culture before you are anything else. Do the work.

A lone human and a lone wolf are contradictions in terms. I am only me in the context of you and us. I cannot be my best or win unless you are doing your best and winning.

Tribe leaders must write and speak

Answer these questions in your journal by really writing them down. Discuss them with at least one of your most important people and really listen to their response.

1. What was the best team you were ever on?

_____
_____
_____

2. What did it feel like when you got together?

_____
_____
_____

3. What was your shared mission and what were your shared values? These may have been unspoken and undefined but they existed.

_____
_____
_____

SUSTAINABLE SUCCESS

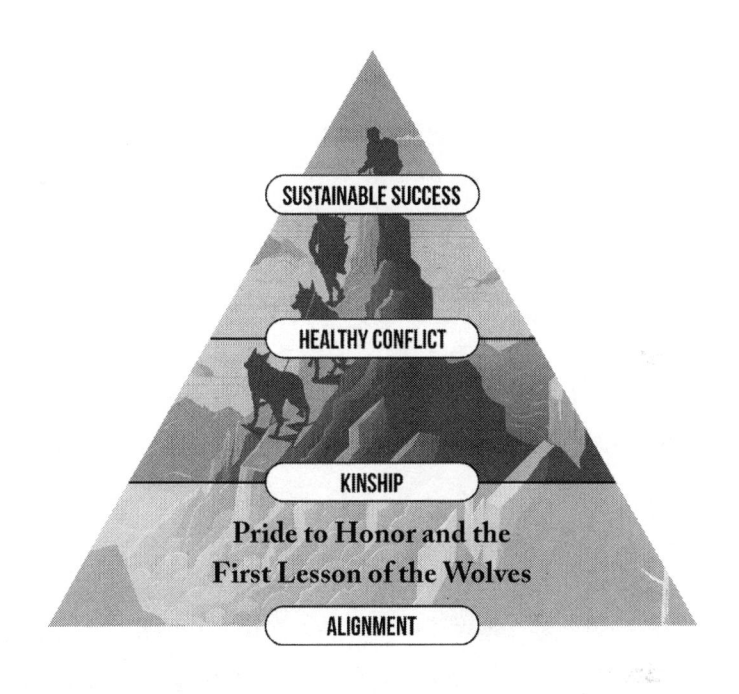

HEALTHY CONFLICT

KINSHIP

Pride to Honor and the
First Lesson of the Wolves

ALIGNMENT

STEP 2 UP THE TRIBE TRIANGLE:

Pride to Honor and the First Lesson of the Wolves

On average, people become leaders of a family or work team at age 30 but don't receive any formal leadership training until age 40. This gap between position and proficiency creates a mistake-filled decade of collateral damage that always comes from on-the-job training and the school of hard knocks. We deserve better and so do our people!

The Tribe Triangle is your instruction manual to fill that gap and intentionally and skillfully create your culture. It begins with some basic knowledge of the two main categories of culture: *pride* and *honor*.

Culture is the operating system of your family or organization. This operating system drives perspective, possibilities, behavior, engagement, risk-taking and just about everything else that humans do when they get together in groups. No wonder culture is the number one lever for organizational performance!

Honor culture is the original OS. It is the shared beliefs and behavior system that was developed over hundreds of thousands of years as we struggled against the epic challenges of life before technology numbed us and dumbed us down.

We are a resilient species designed to struggle successfully against truly awesome adversity. We must remember that our core operating system is built to survive a world where predators literally hunted and ate us. We lived in an apocalyptic era of ice age freezing and flooding and did this with stone age tools. We are built to endure all of this in addition to starvation, with almost no technology beyond wood, stone and fire. Our true technology and the great competitive advantage *was culture technology*.

Culture, unlike hardwired animal drives contains adaptation. Culture can change and it must be taught. Over time this taught culture is refined into a series of traditions that carry across generations and these behaviors ensure the success and survival of the tribe and our species. When we look at the cultures of indigenous peoples there is a set of common beliefs and behaviors that are universal. We call those beliefs and behaviors an *honor-based* culture.

Honor culture is intentionally designed as a group strategy to win in challenging, adverse environments. It contains every best practice of leadership and success in the playbook including engagement, retention, innovation and resiliency. Creating your Honor-Based culture is your roadmap for sustainable success in your family and at work.

The core pillar of Honor is *duty* to the tribe and the members of the tribe. This duty is the responsibility and service to something larger than ourselves. The core principle of duty drives accountability and the indispensable need for a shared vision to work towards. It also requires a shared set of values to dictate group norms and behavior as well as a common mission to collaborate on. These three components, *shared vision, values and mission* are the foundation of every sustainably successful culture in history.

Long ago, all cultures were honor cultures because all people belonged to a family or tribe. We are built for honor and it feels good to be part of. Honor cultures inherently contain a sense of belonging because we are part of a cohesive shared culture that is bigger than ourselves. This sense of belonging drives resiliency, morale and all of the performance levers of successful teams.

Honor cultures contain kinship. This specific behavior requires training and it is not free and it is not easy. To participate in honor culture, we must sacrifice many things that are considered very important in today's world. Some of these things include instant gratification, self-importance and the idea that our lives are the center of the world and reality. In a nutshell, honor culture requires an initiation into service.

Initiation is the ancient tradition of making someone a member of something special. It involves increased status as well as increased responsibilities. It also involves the separation from a past identity of self-gratification and replaced with responsibility and duty for the tribe. In many ways, initiation is the uncomfortable transition from self to service and the process of maturity. Becoming a parent may be the ultimate form of initiation with leadership a close second.

Honor is the highest performing, most fulfilling and resilient culture available. This is proven by every championship sports team that makes individual sacrifices and the 'extra pass' to achieve the big team trophy at the end of the year. It is also demonstrated by every successful family, military unit or work team that makes individual sacrifices for the good of the whole. This is the ancient echo of tribe.

The tribe culture of honor is deeply intimate. The feeling of belonging and meaning is something that all people want back if they had it and dream about it if they didn't. That intimacy of tribe culture is also its undoing.

Tribe culture is limited by size. Tribes are inherently small and intimate and that is the source of their strength. People know each other deeply and are well aware of their strengths and their weaknesses. Accountability is immediate and easy because missions are shared and transparent. Mistakes are obvious and corrected and so are victories which are celebrated. Everyone is seen, important and belongs.

All of this kinship fades then disappears when the group grows past the size of intimate, authentic relationships. For some teams this happens at 20 people. For some 120, but it will happen and it happened with us a species with the event of agriculture then the industrial revolution. Now in the information age we are almost completely pride-based to the point that we even date and work remotely. How did we get here?

When we invented farming and livestock long ago, we solved the core challenge of food and our tribes became villages. The villages beat back the predators and we solved that threat and our villages became cities. Eventually our technology overcame all of our survival needs and we became a global culture and tribe was lost. The death of intimate honor culture created a new culture focused on the individual and that is known as *Pride Culture*. We were all born into pride culture and we all can feel that something important has been lost. That thing is tribe.

> *"It is no measure of health to be well adapted to a profoundly sick society."*
> *-Krishna Murti*

When tribe was lost so were our initiation rituals and now maturity is elusive and unsubstantial as is the meaning and purpose of life that only comes from service.

When tribe was lost so was the resiliency of kinship and belonging and mental health continues to plummet.

When tribe was lost so was the collective, collaborative reciprocity that allows us to hunt the big game of significance. Work without meaning leads to people disengaging and only 20% of people in Western culture are fully engaged and committed to their jobs.

When we lost tribe, we became a society of lost, lone wolves.

Remember 'Ubuntu' which means 'I am because we are and we are because I am?" Sounds a lot like the Law of the wolf pack in Kipling's Jungle book, right? "The strength of the wolf is the pack and the strength of the pack is the wolf." In the wolf world there are no long-term lone wolves. A lone wolf is either looking for a pack or they are starving to death.

The idea of the self-reliant, independent, lone wolf hero is a lie that has been sold to us for generations. At our very core we are interdependent, collaborative and reciprocal pack hunters. Wolves and humans are biologically very different but behaviorally and culturally we are almost identical. It's no wonder the wolf is our first animal ally dating back 35,000 years!

A lone wolf without a pack has the same life and destiny as the lone human without a tribe. We may not be literally starving to death but if you are aware of the terrifying downward trend of clinical depression, anxiety, addiction and suicide you can see that we are starving for the belonging and resiliency that only comes from the kinship of honor culture.

Transforming pride culture into honor culture doesn't mean we shouldn't be as good of an individual as we can or that we aren't unique and sovereign people. We are all those things, however, at some point every facet of our life will involve the collaboration with other people. In these times we have focused too much on what our tribe and society should do for us and too little on what we should do for tribe and society.

Reclaiming Ubuntu is reclaiming Honor.

Tribe leaders must write and speak

There have been times on really bad teams when the pride culture was so strong that you were forced to be a lone wolf to survive. What was one of those teams?

On that pride-based team how did you deal with individual failures and group defeats? How did the team respond to individuals trying to improve the culture?

_____
_____
_____

People don't leave jobs they leave bad managers. On that bad, pride-based team what behavior did the leaders model and what was the effect of that behavior?

_____
_____
_____

SUSTAINABLE SUCCESS
HEALTHY CONFLICT
KINSHIP
Alignment and Becoming the Falconer
Who Brings the Others Home
ALIGNMENT

STEP 3 UP THE TRIBE TRIANGLE:

Alignment and Becoming the Falconer who Brings the Others Home

"Turning and turning in the widening gyre

The falcon cannot hear the falconer;

Things fall apart; the centre cannot hold;"

-William Butler Yeats

You, tribe leader, are the falconer and your people are the falcons that need to hear you so you can bring them home through the storm. You are the falconer who calls forth order from the spinning gyre of chaos and you do this by creating alignment. Alignment is the 'centre' that must hold so things don't fall apart.

Alignment is the foundation of every aspect of culture and your ability to understand and create alignment will define your legacy as a leader in your family and work team.

Alignment trumps talent and it crushes character because those are individual traits and an aligned team will always beat any individual so completely that it's not even fair.

Alignment is the honey that calls in all the lone wolves and talented individuals and it's the glue that holds them together in a collaborative way that is greater than the sum of their parts.

Alignment is your competitive advantage and the very beginning of your trip up the Tribe Triangle.

Alignment consists of three primary parts: vision, values and mission. We are going to go into a deep dive into these three components because they literally will dictate the operating system of your culture, however you need to know your place in this journey. You are The Falconer and you are The One to hold the center to bring your falcons home. The Greek philosopher Heraclitus said it best in his quote on battle:

"Out of every 100 men, ten shouldn't even be there, 80 are just targets, 9 are the real fighters, and we are lucky to have them, for they make the battle. Ah, but the 1, he is a warrior, and he will bring the others back."— Heraclitus

The '10 that shouldn't even be there' are the falcons in your life who are chasing instant gratification and pleasure. They are lost in the "turning and turning of the widening gyre" (tornado) of distraction and addiction. These lost, juvenile souls have no place in your Tribe until they evolve out of that adolescent state. Unfortunately, that will mean rock bottom for many of them.

Regardless of how many well-meaning resources you pour into these falcons they are not ready to start the journey up your Tribe Triangle. They will not be able to share alignment with you because your path of purpose requires a measure of sacrifice and discipline they do not currently possess. In any team there are underperforming, even toxic people that undermine your leadership agendas and the sustainable success of the team. Once you have established the alignment phase of your Tribe Triangle you will notice that these people will self-select out. Wish them well.

The 80 on the battlefield of society that are 'just targets' are the falcons who have elevated their life past pleasure and are now pursuing happiness. These are good people but pursing happiness is ultimately a self-serving venture. In addition, happiness, like pleasure, is dictated by external events that determine the experience of these people. Chasing happiness is like grabbing water; the harder we grip the less we get.

People who are trying to 'be happy' are often deeply unhappy and unfulfilled because sustainable feelings of well-being only come from service to people and projects that are larger than ourselves. This is the ancient and bitter truth pill in every wisdom source in history.

These masses of good people may be part of your community but they will never be part of your honor-based tribe because they haven't advanced to the understanding that the pursuit of service and meaning is the only path that makes the adversity of life make sense and provides fulfillment.

The 9 "real fighters" are your falcons. They are the ones whom "we are lucky to have for they make the battle". Realize that the battle that Heraclitus was really talking about was not a conflict against other armies but a struggle against chaos itself. This is your battle. Whether it be holding the center of your family together through adversity or guiding your work team to freedom and meaning this is war that has come to your gates.

You are 'the one' to bring the others back. You are the tribe leader who will bring all the lone-wolf falcons spinning through the pride-based storm back home to the belonging and success of kinship.

Are you ready to put on that heavy mantle? I propose that if you are reading this, you are. You have been called to lead and the call itself is your qualification. If you are willing, the map is waiting. That road map to tribe begins with creating alignment for your people. In a recent study by LSA Global they discovered that aligned companies are 72% more profitable and increase revenue 58% faster than similar but less aligned organizations. Alignment is the foundation of your success as well as your culture.

As we begin to intentionally create that rock-solid foundation of your tribe, we will start in the next chapter with the big question: why does your tribe exist? This question unlocks the lighthouse of your family or work team and that guiding north star is known as vision.

Tribe leaders must write and speak

Who are the '9 fighters' in your life that 'make the battle'?

_____

_____

_____

You probably don't feel like a real Tribe Leader. Most of us don't and there is an inadequacy-driven imposter syndrome hidden deep in all of us. You are absolved. Remember this: leadership is action not position. Can you own that you have actions you can take to pull your tribe together? Share this vulnerable truth with your 9 real fighters. You'll be surprised by their response.

_____

_____

_____

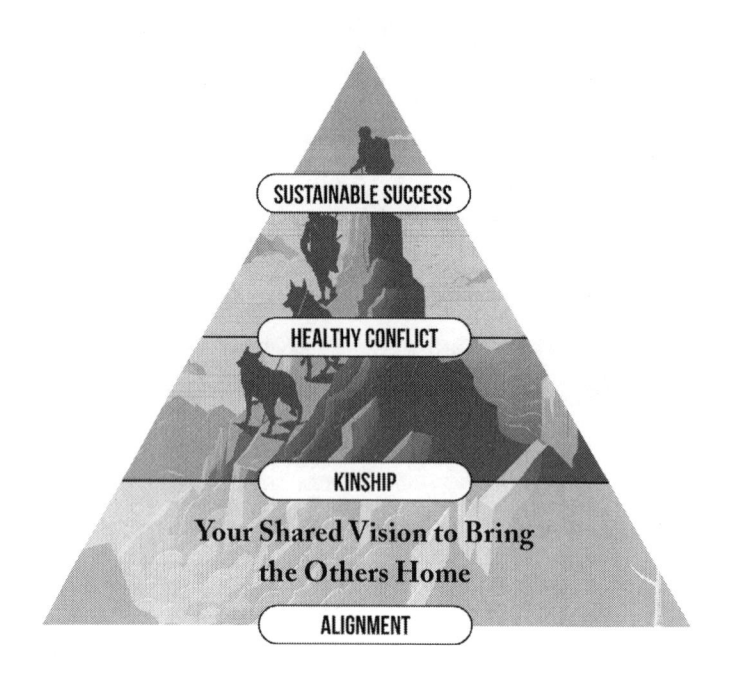

```
        SUSTAINABLE SUCCESS

        HEALTHY CONFLICT

           KINSHIP
    Your Shared Vision to Bring
         the Others Home
          ALIGNMENT
```

STEP 4 UP THE TRIBE TRIANGLE:

Your Shared Vision Brings the Others Home

Your vision is not a luxury, it is a necessity.
It is the pillar of smoke by day and fire by night that guides
us through the desert.

Establishing a powerful North Star for your tribe attracts, engages and retains the best people. It is also how you can get the best *from* them and *for* them. Your vision is the lighthouse of your culture. The brighter and more powerful it is, the more it will guide and protect your collective journey when nights are the darkest.

Whether it be family or faction, your vision is *why* your group exists. I recommend you dig deep into this initial question because a shallow *why*, such as money or pleasure, is a shallow vision and that will be inadequate to attract, inspire and guide your tribe, especially when things get stormy and uncertain. And they will. Below are some techniques and best practices to discover and establish a powerful vision for your tribe.

The 5 Whys

Using the Japanese strategy of the *5 Whys* is a great technique for beginning to excavate your powerful shared vision. This process consists of asking a series of iterative questions to dig down to the root of an issue. Here is an example of a corporate *5 Why* process so you can see how it works. Do this collectively and verbally.

First Why: Why does your company exist? Often the initial answer to this is to provide a service or sell a product. Good start. Practical, but not strong enough to attract and maintain powerful wolves to your pack and guide them into engagement and retention when things get hard.

Second Why: Why is it important that we sell the product (or whatever you do)? The answer to this second why is 'to make money'. This is a better, deeper and more honest answer. Wolves like money.

Third Why: Why is it important to make money? Because otherwise we will go out of business and no one will have jobs. This is even more powerful because it speaks to the fact that underneath the comfort and technology of our current world there is still the fear of starvation and a drive to survive and thrive.

Fourth Why. Why are those jobs important? Because, behind all those employees are families and communities that count on our company for a livelihood. Now you are speaking to all those lone wolves about pack and community and things that are larger than themselves. When you start to share your vision of caring about a service greater than self, you and your culture are just one step away from purpose and meaning.

We have now landed at the real vision of the company: to support the employees, families and communities that surround it. This is a vastly more powerful, engaging and long-lasting purpose than just selling products and making money. AND you still have one more *Why* to go…

This shared awareness of service becomes part of the engagement, innovation, morale and retention strategy for employees as well a vital part of the company's brand that is reflected in marketing and client relations.

This 5 *Why* technique works with parenting, vacations, education and just about anything else humans do together and need to drill down into a deeper motivation and truth. And that's what vision really is.

Vision as inspiration

A powerful vision is aspirational and inspirational. Establishing this ambitious destination is one of the most important jobs you have as tribe leader.

"Leaders are dealers in hope." -Napoleon Bonaparte

A powerful vision galvanizes the hopeful and optimistic person inside all of us. An aspirational vision is irresistible to high-drive humans which are the ones you really want in your pack and on your team.

Your aspirational vision does not have to be specific in a granular way or even particularly realistic. This is why mythology and inspiration work; we all have a powerful ability to suspend disbelief when it comes to *story* and vision is a story at its core. Holy Grail, heaven, Valhalla, championships, curing cancer are all visions that have captivated and engaged people across time.

One of the most powerful examples of the power of an

aspirational vision in my career as a culture consultant was working with a management team at SpaceX. On the wall of the boardroom we were working in were two giant, round, globe-like maps. One of the maps was a beautiful, blue-green Earth planet and the other, a cracked and desolate Mars.

During our conversation about vision, the Space X leader pointed to the globes and said, "That's *our* vision."

"I get it" I said, "we're going to Mars."

He stood puzzled for a moment and then looked at me carefully and said, "look at the maps again." I did, and saw that the blue green planet was not Earth, it was a terraformed, blue-green Mars. Space X is not going *to* mars. Space X is going to *get us mars.*

The hair still stands up on my arms when I tell that story because it perfectly demonstrates the power of an aspirational vision. I wanted to be part of that team and part of that epic goal. Make sure your vision is BIG enough to feed a family, support a community and power a career. This is how you make a dent in the universe.

No one accidentally walks uphill. No one inadvertently climbs a mountain. Success is not casual and it is not random. It is a product of relentless will following a steep, long and arduous path towards an aspirational vision. It also creates light in the darkness.

Vision as lighthouse

Things are going to get hard this year. There will be setbacks, doubt and adversity. Vision is your tribe's anchor to the meaning that lets us see that the suffering of life make sense.

We've all heard Nietzsche's quote that "When a man's *why* is strong enough, he can bear almost any how." This is the definition of resiliency and all the primary pillars of resiliency come from a sense of belonging and service to something larger than ourselves. Vision is the source of that *why.*

When the Jews escaped from the bondage and tyranny of Egypt they headed out to the Promised Land. What they did not expect was the trip through the desert. You will face a similar challenge when embarking on your quest for a high performing team. The desert is a hard and unforgiving place. There is an old Arabic parable that the desert exists to test the faithful and it will. What enabled the Jews to navigate their years in the desert was following a pillar of smoke by day and a pillar of fire by night. These pillars were their vision.

Like all treasure, aspirational, shared visions are not easy to find. Here are a few places to start.

Tribe leaders must write and speak

If money were no object and you could not fail, what would you be doing with your life? This exercise will free you from objective and realistic goals and liberate an aspirational vision for your life. Can you be that brave for your family and work team?

_____

_____

_____

What are the important priorities your family or work team is focused on and why?

Ask 'why' to the answer to that question.
Ask why to the next 3 answers as well and you will have arrived at a much deeper purpose, drive or maybe even the meaning of life.

_____

_____

_____

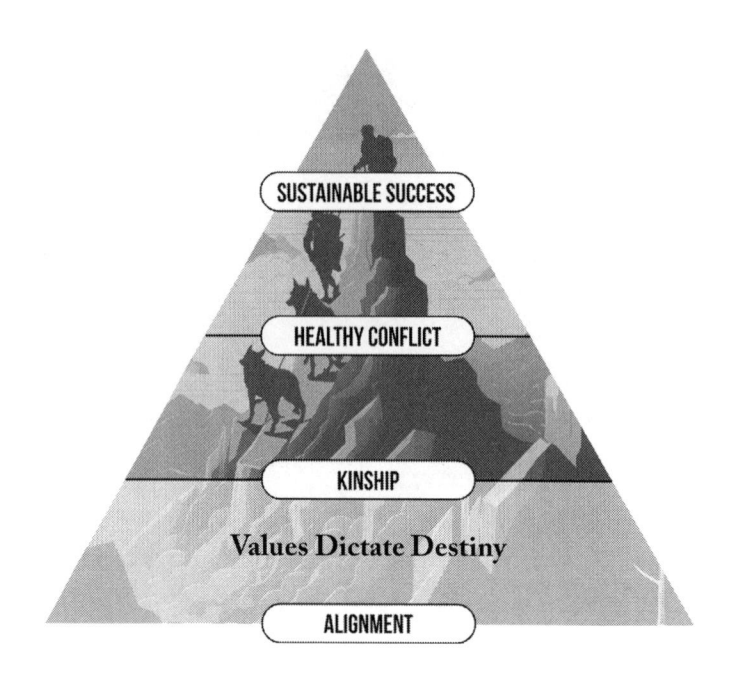

STEP 5 UP THE TRIBE TRIANGLE:

Values Dictate Destiny

"*Character is destiny.*" –Heraclitus

Your personal values will ultimately define your destiny. These values will also dictate the quality of the life you lead while getting to that destiny. The quality of that journey may be even more important than the destination.

In addition, as Tribe Leader of your family and work team, your personal values also have a massive impact on the journey and destination your people have in their lives. Remember, you are the Head of Culture before you are anything else and if you are not clear with your personal core values, your team will not have a chance to get clarity on the shared values that will guide their behavior.

Values really do drive our personal destiny as well as the destiny of our people and projects. We are duty-bound to put some love and time into exploring and discovering what these values are and how they work.

Let's start with what values are. Values are the principles and priorities that drive our behaviors. They literally direct the actions of our lives. Values dictate actions because they establish the internal hierarchy of priorities we have inside of us at any given moment.

It is estimated that adults make about 35,000 decisions a day. Most are tiny and seemingly inconsequential but many are literally career and life defining. When we are faced with one of these endless moments of choice, we must have an internal engine of judgment that makes us decide one decision over another. The decision that wins is always the one that aligns to the strongest operating value happening *at that moment with the choices available to us.* You may want to read that last sentence again.

People always make their best decisions

This is a common axiom in the study of economics (which is really the science of decision-making not the science of money). When I first heard that shared by a professor, I strongly (and unfortunately vocally) disagreed. If you're hearing that 'people always make their best decisions' for the first time, I'll bet you disagree with it to.

"People always make their best decisions?! Are you crazy? People make terrible decisions all the time!" Well, let's dig a little deeper.

Remember, people make decisions based on their loudest value operating *at the moment*.

Take breakfast for example. Let's look at a couple values that often come into play in deciding what to eat:

- *Expedience* might be an important value because we don't want to be late for work.
- *Health* may be another because we all know that breakfast is the most important meal of the day.
- *Delicious* is right up there too, right? After all, we're all sugar-loving primates at our core.

So, what did *you* have for breakfast today? You ended up eating whatever the available choice was that aligned with your loudest value *at the moment*. Even though we all value *health* we have all eaten sugary junk in spite of the obvious knowledge that it wasn't our healthiest choice. We ate the junky cereal because it was our most delicious choice.

If we are distracted or too tired to hold our highest values at the top of the value hierarchy and if no one is holding us accountable then the lower, base values will bob to the top like ancient animal buoys. We have all committed and declared that we are not going to do something and ended up doing that very thing.

Values will always fulfil immediate gratification so it is vital that we establish long term goals as desirable *now* in the short term. It's the only way you can maintain these uncomfortable and challenging value-based behavior upgrades. There are many ways to do this.

Firstly, we can bank on the immediate dopamine hit that we receive when we make disciplined choices. Teach yourself and train yourself that dopamine feels good and therefor discipline feels good.

Secondly, oxytocin and serotonin are two other feel-good hormones that are released by *celebrating* long-term decisions especially when others notice and praise our powerful choices. Hang out with disciplined people who support and celebrate each other and that will go a long way in helping you hold your higher values. Those rare people who truly want the best for you do it because you are a part of *them*. Those people are *tribe*. That honorable behavior is your character, reputation and brand. Going public with your core values is a great way to receive accountability for your high-value decisions.

Values are lethal and they not free

Values drive the decision-making engine of our lives and every decision has a cost. **Big decisions have big costs and choosing is refusing.** The word decide contains the same Latin root as the words homicide, insecticide and suicide. That root 'cide' means to cut or kill.

De-ciding is killing off our other options. This is incredibly important because those other options are often very valuable and their death is often very painful. Especially the big ones. For example, deciding to enter a relationship is not free. It inherently kills off some of our other choices such as independence and freedom.

When we move into Tribe Leader category, our value-based decisions need to be very intentional. We also need to be very sober about the cost of our decisions and the lifestyle and discipline skills that will empower us to keep making those hard choices for the long journey. We need values and decisions to go far not fast.

Leaders are people whose decisions affect other people. The ability to make powerful long-term decisions now is the greatest skill we can develop as leaders. Develop and claim this skill for your tribe and your life or someone else will. You deserve the results of those big-value decisions. Your people and projects demand it.

Tribe leaders must write and speak

Step 1: What are 5 of your core values? Notice that the very act of deciding on 5 from the list is costing you the other values you are not choosing. *Choosing is refusing and deciding is killing. This is the price of being a Tribe Leader.*

1. Core Value _____
2. Core Value _____
3. Core Value _____
4. Core Value _____
5. Core Value _____

Accountability	Connection	Travel
Achievement	Contentment	Dignity
Adaptability	Contribution	Diversity
Adventure	Cooperation	Environment
Altruism	Courage	Efficiency
Ambition	Creativity	Equality
Authenticity	Curiosity	Ethics
Balance	Perseverance	Excellence
Beauty	Personal	Fairness
Being the best	Fulfillment	Faith
Belonging	Power	Family
Career	Pride	Financial stability
Caring	Recognition	Forgiveness
Collaboration	Reliability	Freedom
Commitment	Respect	Friendship
Community	Responsibility	Fun
Compassion	Risk-taking	Future generations
Competence	Safety	Generosity
Confidence	Security	Giving back

Grace	Thrift	Nature
Gratitude	Tradition	Openness
Growth	Humor	Optimism
Harmony	Inclusion	Order
Health	Independence	Parenting
Home	Initiative	Patience
Honesty	Integrity	Patriotism
Hope	Intuition	Peace
Humility	Job security	Trust
Self-discipline	Joy	Truth
Self-expression	Justice	Understanding
Self-respect	Kindness	Uniqueness
Serenity	Knowledge	Vision
Service	Leadership	Vulnerability
Simplicity	Learning	Wealth
Spirituality	Legacy	Well-being
Sportsmanship	Leisure	Wholeheartedness
Stewardship	Love	Wisdom
Success	Loyalty	Time
Teamwork	Making a difference	

Step 2: Clarify your top 5 core values down to 3 by cutting and killing off the 2 least important. Scribe the remaining 3 core values below.

1. Core Value _____
2. Core Value _____
3. Core Value _____

What does it feel like to make this sacrifice?

_____
_____
_____

What is your thought process and priorities in making this de-*ciding?*

_____

_____

_____

Step 3: Determine the price of your value-driven life so you can pay it.

There are sacrifices required when using those 3 core values as your deciding priorities. For example, the value **growth** will cost you stability, comfort and control. The value **service** will cost you freedom and the values **vitality** and **health** will cost you pleasure. What are the costs of your three core values? If you can't see the cost now just wait. You will.

Cost of Core Value 1 _____

Cost of Core Value 2 _____

Cost of Core Value 3 _____

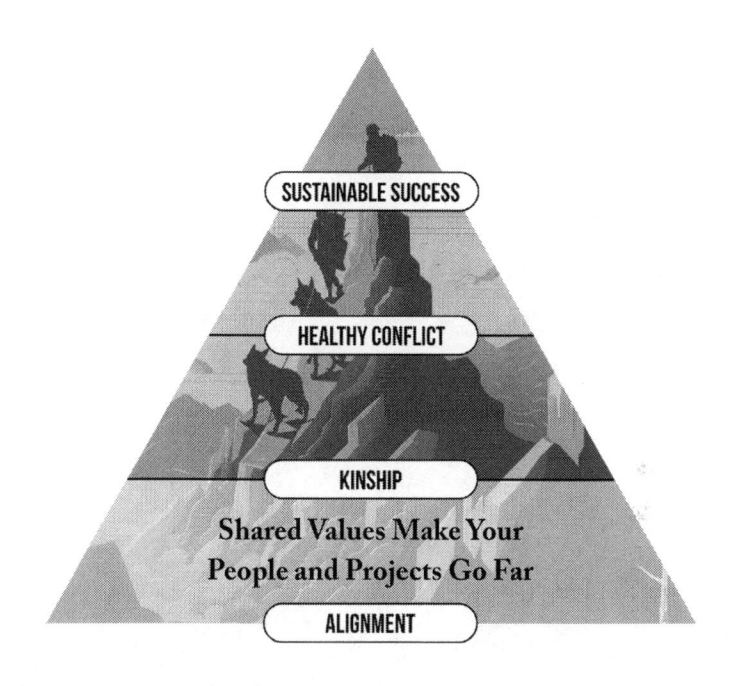

STEP 6 UP THE TRIBE TRIANGLE:

Shared Values Make Your People and Projects Go Far

"If you want to go fast, go alone.
If you want to go far, go together."
—African Proverb

Individual values define our actions, character and destiny. Collective values do the same thing for families, teams and tribes. Values are the rudders, guardrails and signposts along the challenging roadmap of culture creation. Values tell us what to do when we don't know what to do and when no one is there to *tell us* what to do.

Without shared values we cannot maintain sustainable high performance which is a universal byproduct of ongoing collaboration and reciprocity. Like individual values, shared group values guide our decisions and the sacrifices those decisions demand from us. All choices command a cost. For an aligned team anything is possible but not *everything* is possible. Choosing is refusing and we all must choose our path.

A family and a team that has shared values are going to share the same moral and operational compass. These values guide us through decision-making, especially decisions that have high costs, tradeoffs and consequences. Families and teams that have no shared values are chaotic, dysfunctional and ultimately unsuccessful.

How do we create a set of shared values from a group of individuals who all have different *individual values?* This is one of the oldest leadership questions and challenges in the history of leadership itself and it has to do with accepting (and ultimately celebrating) the differences of people while being able to form alignment with them. We will never be able to share *beliefs* with everyone but we can always find *agreement*. This is the core of kinship.

The shared values that drive group behaviors are known as norms. These are the collective actions that are expected and accepted by the tribe. Leaders are the primary drivers of these value-based behaviors due to their position. There are many strategies for creating these group decisions and being skillful and intentional with these choices is a core competency of leaders. Below are the three main group decision-making strategies.

Group decisions by position

This is the quickest and most efficient strategy but very risky for you, Tribe Leader because you are the ultimate dictator of direction and you will inevitably reap all the glory as well as all the blame. This can also be highly disruptive to your tribe because with every wrong decision they will have to determine if your leadership is safe and successful which brings substantial instability. In addition, because this decision-making strategy does not integrally include other people, it often fails to benefit from the different perspectives, experiences and personalities of others that can expand options and statistically get better results.

If you make the right decision you get glory. If you make the wrong decision you shoulder the entire blame. Too many of these wrong decisions is not good for the tribe and it is definitely not good for you because it erodes your authority and creates a blast radius of chaos throughout the tribe.

Implement this strategy when you need speed and decisive action and get as much feedback from the tribe as possible.

Group decision by majority

This strategy takes longer than decision by position and is therefore less efficient and often less decisive. It also is statistically more successful because it involves more data, options, experience and everything else that comes from human diversity.

Winston Churchill famously said, "Democracy is the worst form of government except for all the others." The democratic decision-making strategy suffers from the same flaw as decision by position; it's great when you're right and terrible when you're wrong. You can see this divisiveness in politics at every level. The minority who losses the vote is quiet when things are going well but the moment the majority makes an error, we inevitably see the knives come out and the grenades being thrown.

Group decision by consensus

This is the most challenging but most stable of the three group decision-making strategies. Not only does it take the longest because it involves the entire group but it also requires the agreement of the entire group. Often this can be almost impossible with larger groups.

The benefit of consensus is it protects the integrity of the group itself. Consensus is safety because when the chosen decision and path is proven incorrect there is no one to blame. There is no collateral damage and no daggers being thrown. When we have a collective failure, we learn and move on. During particularly challenging times this technique can be the glue that holds the tribe together and be the difference between resiliency and dissolution.

Remember, *consensus is agreement not belief.* People can have their differences in belief be honored but still agree with the group. I strongly recommend you practice the consensus-building skill set and that begins by honoring the different beliefs of others then asking them to join you in agreement for the sake of the group. **You will be amazed what people will be willing to do for the group when their personal beliefs are seen and honored.**

Often, people will abstain from active agreement and support in order to throw 'I told you so' grenades later. These people are petty, adolescent and toxic to the tribe. One technique to quickly capture these people is to reframe your consensus statement from "does everyone agree?" to "does anyone *not* agree?" Anyone abstaining from agreement by abstaining from participating will have automatically agreed. You may need to read that again.

Values drive decisions and we need collective values for collective decisions. This is the very core of collaboration and kinship. This form of agreement that holds the group together for the sake of the whole operates in many other communal animal species.

> *If you want to go fast go alone.*
> *If you want to go far, go together."*
> *-African Proverb*

A powerful lesson from the decision-making of deer.

It is commonly believed that the alpha doe of a deer herd makes the decisions that the herd follows but this is not entirely the case. Deer, like many other communal species, use a much more democratic and collective decision-making strategy.

Like wolves and humans, deer *can* live alone but must be in groups to thrive. Also, like wolves, the deer leader is a powerful matriarchal female who teaches the young deer necessary survival skills and holds the social unit together.

When a herd of deer arrive at a decision that affects the group, for example choosing between two water or food sources, the deer stand and face the direction they are choosing to go. When the herd reaches a critical mass of over 50% facing the same direction the alpha doe will lead the herd in that direction. Agreement is made and the power and safety of alignment is maintained.

The same is true for teams and tribes. **We vote with our actions in the same way we vote with our dollars and our ballots.** Successful leaders are very aware of the collective behavior of their tribe and customers and they lead accordingly. Hold the group together with shared value-driven actions so your tribe can go far and not just fast.

Tribe leaders must write and speak

Your tribe values are derived from the actions that are in alignment with a path towards your shared vision. Using the list from Step 5, what are 3 core values that dictate behaviors that will move your tribe towards your vision?

Shared Vision _____
Shared Value 1 _____
Shared Value 2 _____
Shared Value 3 _____

These 3 shared tribe values are not free and all contain an opportunity cost of another behavior even if that is just in the short term. For example, *Customer Service* as a shared value contains the short-term opportunity costs of *efficiency, time and profit*. As a tribe leader you must be aware of these costs and be prepared to champion the act of paying them. What is a sacrifice that must be paid for each of your shared tribe values?

Sacrifice for shared value 1 _____
Sacrifice for shared value 2 _____
Sacrifice for shared value 3 _____

Your shared tribe values may be different than your individual values, however they should not be the actual sacrifice that is required for your shared tribe values!

If those individual and shared values are in opposition then this is the time to pause and take a deep look at your personal vision and values (which are connected) as well as your shared tribe vision and values.

Something will have to give and sometimes it is time for old stories to die for new ones to be born.

Any conflicts here _____

SUSTAINABLE SUCCESS

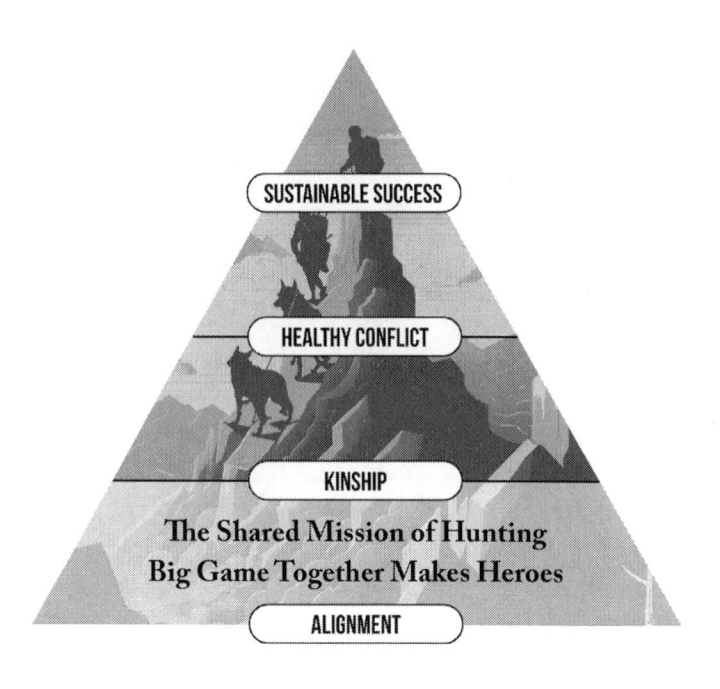

HEALTHY CONFLICT

KINSHIP

The Shared Mission of Hunting
Big Game Together Makes Heroes

ALIGNMENT

STEP 7 UP THE TRIBE TRIANGLE:

Shared Missions of Hunting Big Game Together Makes Heroes

"There is no delight in owning anything unshared."
— *Seneca*

Everything of significance comes from the active collaboration of people working together on a shared mission. This does not negate the celebration of individual accomplishments. In fact, *collective* challenges augment the prestige of *individual* accomplishment because it provides a shared platform on which individuals can distinguish themselves and be celebrated.

We only achieve personal glory by being witnessed and lionized by our tribe in the context of achievements made in the pursuit of service *to* the tribe. Individual triumphs that are not shared are actually dismissed by the group which ends up denying the individual the recognition that all people value and many people demand.

Acknowledgment by the group is one of the most potent drivers for individual engagement and retention. This is even more true when the acknowledgment comes from *you*, Tribe Leader. **Give praise liberally because it is probably the one form of currency in your budget that you have an endless amount of. Be generous!**

A shared mission in an honor-based culture is the root of heroism and greatness. People will always do more for others within their kinship systems than for themselves. Who would you truly sacrifice something of great value for? Whom would you sacrifice your *life* for? This is an easy answer for men and women who are or have been in an honor-based culture.

Athletes in dedicated team sports report being willing to sacrifice their individual health for their team. This is especially true when the collective mission at stake is significant such as a championship game where everyone plays hurt if need be. Championships are literally hunting *Big Game*.

Mothers and fathers also regularly make unfathomable sacrifices of time, resources and even their personal dreams and even lives for their children. These are heroic acts that we parents would never make for our co-workers.

Soldiers too, are willing to sacrifice their personal well-being and lives in the service of their brothers and sisters. Once you have experienced a culture of aligned collective mission that activates heroic behavior the rest of the world begins to look very shallow. Is it any wonder that only 27% of Americans report being fully engaged in their jobs? We are designed to be so much more but this can only be activated in a Tribe Culture.

A shared mission opens up the scope and scale of the projects and prey we can hunt, but it also actually makes the individuals within the tribe operate at higher levels. We are literally better wolves when we are embedded in an aligned pack and hunting collective big game together. **If you want to live at hero level and raise others to that level as well, find or create a tribe and serve!**

Collective success is built on individuals being successful. Conversely, individuals can only be sustainably successful on a successful team. This is true in sports, business, the military and in your family. Again, Ubuntu, which will be an endless, ancient mantra repeated on the path of creating and maintaining Tribe. *I am because we are, and we are because I am.* They are as connected as the two sides of the same coin.

The strength of the pack is the wolf and the strength of the wolf is the pack. Without the pack there is no opportunity for big game glory and therefor no opportunity for individual accomplishment. Lone wolves ingloriously hunt rabbits and scavenge.

No one remembers who won the Oscar for best actor, but they know the movies. No one remembers the richest people in the world, but they know the companies. No one remembers the scoring leader in any year, but they remember the team that wins the championship.

A shared mission in an honor-based culture drives engagement, competitiveness and retention because it unlocks **significance and meaning.** Set your north star of vision then set your course of shared mission goals towards that promised land.

Let's build a rocket.
Let's go to space.
Let's go to mars.
Let's go get mars.

The Roadmap of Tribe Triangle Alignment

A map is a symbol for objects or ideas in the real world that are too big or too complex to fully grasp or share. For example, globes are maps of our vast planet that is too big to fully grasp. Calendars, schedules and clocks are maps of time which is too complex to fully understand. Shared maps enable us to collaborate on big, complex game we may not fully grasp or understand but still need to engage with. Maps are a hidden superpower of humanity.

The Tribe Triangle is the map of culture creation and your time-tested roadmap for gathering the lone wolves into an aligned pack capable of hunting Big Game and thriving.

Using any map successfully involves two things: *navigation* and *route-finding*. Successfully implementing group missions involve the same two components.

Navigation is the big picture, 20,000-foot overview of the terrain. Navigating on our map is the shared vision for the future. It is the direction or azimuth of where we are going. This is the Big Game we are ultimately hunting and without this we are lost and unable to navigate our long-term journey. Big game should be aspirational which makes it inspirational.

When we chunk down our big, hairy, audacious vision into manageable targets they are called goals. Goals are also Big Game but achievable ones. Goals are the successive bridges we cross on the endless path toward our vision. This is the act of route-finding which is actually walking the path. This is where we spend most of our time.

We pull the map of vision out to navigate when we start our day and end our day to make sure we are on the right path. We might need to return to our shared vision more often when the path is obscured or challenging but remember, the map is not the real world. It is only a crude symbol representing the real world. We must walk that journey in real time with real projects and real people. Those people and projects are our shared missions and both need to be seen and appreciated.

Tribe leaders must write and speak

Who are 3 important members of your tribe that would shine with more praise or appreciation from you, Tribe Leader?

1. _____
2. _____
3. _____

What is a heroic behavior of personal sacrifice (however small or great) that you demonstrate that comes from the service to something greater than yourself?

_____
_____
_____

Who are the people that heroic behavior serves?

_____
_____
_____

What is an important larger shared mission that you can have your team recommit to that will bring forth more of their heroic behavior?

_____
_____
_____

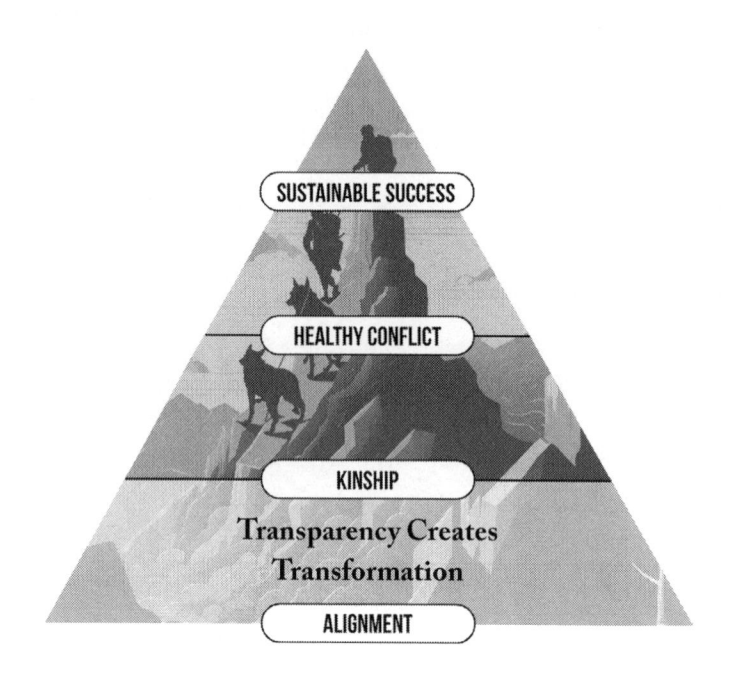

STEP 8 UP THE TRIBE TRIANGLE:

Transparency Creates Transformation

"A lack of transparency results in distrust and a deep sense of insecurity."
–Dali Lama

Transparency is the central pillar of your tribe's Shared Mission which is a primary component in your foundation of alignment. Transparency is one of the most effective (and cost effective) ways to accelerate performance in your culture as well as a being a powerful lever that increases profit and measurable success.

Transparency drives success in numerous ways including increased collaboration, accountability, resiliency, engagement and retention. You need all these culture components to have a sustainably thriving tribe. We can divide the impact of transparency into two categories: People and Projects. Both are vital for your mission and your culture to thrive.

Transparency Powers People

Transparency increases trust and credibility which are central culture drivers of engagement and retention. When we freely share information in a way that benefits the tribe as a whole as well as the tribe's individuals, we have transparency. When we embed openness in the foundation of our culture, we instill trust.

Transparent leaders and organizations are viewed as more trustworthy and this not only powers engagement, retention and commitment but risk-taking as well. In the large-scale Edelman Trust Barometer study it was found that almost 40% of people don't trust their employer and we need to do better in our tribe!

> *"Transparency is the currency of trust."*
> *-Frida Lewis-Hall MD, CMO, Pfizer*

Another culture outcome of transparency are feelings of certainty and *fairness*. These are two of the major psychological drivers of people in all social arenas but especially ones involving emotions and money (such as families and careers). When your team (or family) feels out of the loop, they have less trust and demonstrate less loyalty to leaders and their team. Certainty and fairness also increase psychological safety and this powers risk-taking, innovation and creativity.

Lack of transparency makes people feel less included and, in many studies, leads to substantial drops in feelings of belonging and social standing. People who experience less belonging feel rejected and often disengage from communities and projects. Less than 30% of Americans report being 'fully engaged' in their jobs and this is a social and economic catastrophe.

Another major factor of transparency is simply people's work being witnessed. Are they being seen? This is a huge component of tribe and a major part of the engine of honor-based cultures. Acknowledgment is a major predictor of employee happiness and cultures that are viewed as more open are seen as more trustworthy and more effective. *You* need to be seen this way, tribe Leader!

Radical transparency not only increases engagement and retention but also helps recruit talent. These forms of transparency can show up as shared goals, visions, promotions and profit sharing or it may simply be openness of sharing celebrations and challenges. Even the exchange of resiliency and stress management practices that come from transparent sharing of members on your team who are frustrated, disengaged and burned out can be a major factor in increasing engagement and morale.

In addition to the host of social and cultural benefits of increased transparency in your tribe are the increases of raw mission success on projects.

Transparency Powers Projects

Increased transparency accelerates collaboration, accountability and ultimately the reciprocity which is the sustainable engine of kinship in your tribe. These are all indispensable components to successful missions.

Transparency accelerates collaboration because when people have more access to the projects happening across the tribe, clan and nation, they have more opportunities to share best practices, experience and insights that will improve the whole project or organization. This is major driver of success and is only activated within tribe cultures of shared missions.

Transparency drives accountability because it triggers honor. People will only do truly heroic things for people in their tribe and will almost always do more for others that they will do for themselves. In addition, transparency drives accountability because it increases trackability and if we can't transparently measure what is happening in our tribe we can't transparently manage it.

We can see the increase of both collaboration and accountability with the implementation of the OKR transparency system that was brought over from Intel to Google.

OKR stands for *Objectives and Key Results,* and is a transparency system at its core. OKR is a system that you can use in your organization even if that work team is currently your family!

The premise of OKRs is to crystalize the goals and objectives of the company or team. More importantly, it is to *make public* the goals of each person on the team.

At Google, each employee from the CEO down to the most recent hire, establish an *Objective and the Key Results* that drive the success of that objective. They do this each quarter and all these OKRs are available on a common, transparent platform. The transparency of this goal and benchmark system makes it possible for others to not only see what everyone is working on (accountability) but also enables them to collaborate on other people's projects that they may have experience or expertise in (collaboration). In addition, seeing what other members of the team are committed to enables everyone to see if their goals and objectives are in alignment which is the very foundation of tribe.

Transparency around themes of mission information, challenges and progress updates must be openly and regularly shared. For the practice of transparency to be embedded in your Tribe's foundation of alignment, you will have to establish some protocol. These practices may seem tedious and repetitive at first but eventually they will be seen as opportunities for celebration and collaboration. Remember, it takes 30 days of sustainable new behavior to form a new habit, 90 days for a new collection of habits (that we call a lifestyle) and up to a year to build your new culture. This is why we are doing the 52 steps!

Transparency powers collaboration which is the superpower of both wolves, humans and every other communal predator on the planet. In the next chapter we explore and discover the techniques of pack hunting the big game of sustainable success.

Tribe leaders must write and speak

What is a project that you are passionate about that you can share with your family or team?

_____
_____
_____

Ask them about a project that they are passionate about.

_____
_____
_____

What is a challenge that you currently have that you are willing to share with your family or team?

_____
_____
_____

Ask them about a challenge that they are currently having.

_____
_____
_____

SUSTAINABLE SUCCESS

HEALTHY CONFLICT

KINSHIP
Reciprocity is the Engine
of Kinship

ALIGNMENT

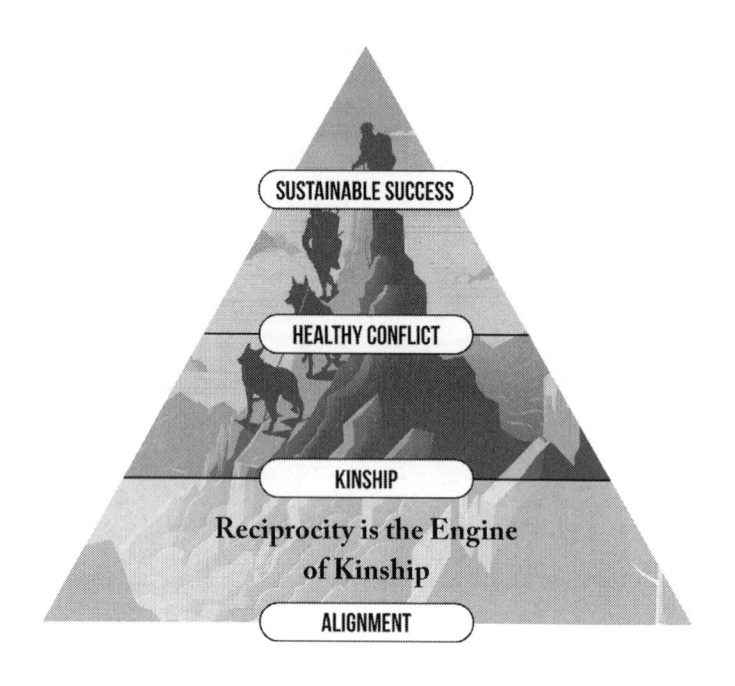

STEP 9 UP THE TRIBE TRIANGLE:

Reciprocity is the Engine of Kinship

"There is one word which may serve as a rule of practice for all one's life–reciprocity."
–Confucius

Reciprocity is one of the main behavioral engines that drives kinship and an honor-based culture. You need this people power-source because without established reciprocity practices in place, members of your family, community or company will begin to disengage and only perform in immediate, transactional ways.

Reciprocity is a downstream creation from your earlier tribe development work of *transparency* and *collaboration*. Remember, transparency drives collaboration in your people and your projects and both transparency and collaboration must be in place for sustainable reciprocity to be created and maintained.

Like all the other components of your foundation of alignment, reciprocity drives behavior of your *people,* quality of your *process* and results of your *projects.*

rec·i·proc·i·ty
/ˌresəˈpräsədē/
noun

1. The practice of exchanging things with others for mutual benefit, especially privileges granted by one organization to another.

Reciprocity is a social norm that involves exchanges between members of a group. It is the agreed upon response to another's action with another equivalent action and denotes a deep interconnection between people who *share a foundation of alignment.*
In Stone Age Economics (1972), anthropologist Marshall Sahlins identified three modes of reciprocity:

- Generalized Reciprocity.
- Balanced Reciprocity.
- Negative Reciprocity.

We are going to explore all three of these forms of reciprocity in relationships because they are the mutual exchange of energy and support between partners. In a nutshell, the three forms of reciprocity are: *Generalized Reciprocity* is giving without expecting an immediate specific outcome. *Balanced Reciprocity* is an immediate equal give-and-take, and *Negative Reciprocity* is the exchange of consequences when boundaries are crossed or agreements are broken (Fehr & Gächter, 2000).

Generalized Reciprocity

In honor-based cultures, Tribe Leaders are not as much concerned about maximizing immediate, measurable net results (like income) but rather about their net giving because gathering a large number of beneficiaries who owe them a reciprocal favor is much more powerful because favors are a universal form of currency and accrue over time. Generalized reciprocity is apparent in functional politics at every level and you can both witness it and *feel it* in your team.

Generalized Reciprocity is a form of investing in the relationships of your people and in your people themselves. This investment has the highest ROI you can make. People breaking this social agreement tear at the very fabric of your team and lead to massive loss of honor and standing. People who do not understand and abide by this form of reciprocity are **toxic takers and will quickly self-select out or be removed from the tribe and you are better off without them** until they learn that Generalized Reciprocity drives the power of networking, socializing and alliance-building and is indispensable for long-term success of themselves as an individual and as part of a tribe.

Tribe Leaders giving attention and mentorship to followers in exchange for commitment and loyalty is also an example of Generalized Reciprocity.

Balanced Reciprocity

Balanced reciprocity is an immediate and equal give and take. It is so core to successful cultures that according to the ancient philosopher,

Seneca: *"Any exchange of gifts or services produce mutual obligations between benefactor and beneficiaries."*

For the good, pride-based people that you are attracting and onboarding into your honor-based culture, this is the easiest form of reciprocity to grasp because it is immediate and simple. It also powers a live and tangible improvement in the three organizational performance pillars of *people, process and project success.*

Balanced Reciprocity Powers People

Balanced Reciprocity powers people because it underscores the fact that in your developing honor-based tribe, people's behaviors are *actually seen and acknowledged.* This makes people feel like they are not just a faceless gear in a machine and that their hard work, attention to detail and care will be witnessed and rewarded. This is the kinship and relationship connections that come from your earlier investment in *transparency and collaboration.* Reciprocity is also a primary driver of **feelings of belonging which are central to the indispensable tribe function of resiliency** which will be a repeated theme the rest of this journey!

Balanced Reciprocity Powers Process

In addition to relationship-based people upgrades of morale and retention, Balanced Reciprocity also drives improvement of *process* because there is an immediate reward for excellence, attention to detail, innovation, *finishing* and all other forms of process success. Balanced reciprocity is the most powerful form of human currency that makes people feel like their investment in a team is paying off.

Balanced Reciprocity Powers Projects

Balanced Reciprocity drives overall project success because it rewards success behaviors in general. Balanced Reciprocity powers all the mission best practices we have developed and are developing because it *actively and immediately rewards them.* Examples of these mission success best practices are *asking for help* (vulnerability), *giving help* (collaboration), *goal setting and implementation* and all the other life skills that are so integral to ongoing project success. Reward your people for project success and you will train them to continue that behavior. Establish that reward system in your whole culture and watch success blossom!

Negative Reciprocity

It is important to note that although reciprocity is usually positive (e.g. returning a favor), it can also be seen as having a short term negative impact (e.g. punishing a negative action). This is not a dynamic that is commonly accepted in today's culture but it is the source of many indispensable tribe norms such as maintaining healthy boundaries, competition, conflict resolution and, most importantly, creating a culture of accountability. We will be getting to all of that later on this journey of culture development when we get to phase 3 of the Tribe Triangle, Healthy Conflict.

Kinship is the engine that sits in the very center of your tribe and honor-based culture. Reciprocity is the engine that powers kinship. Reciprocity is indispensable for building and maintaining this rare and high-performing form of culture and has an extremely high ROI. Invest early and often, Tribe Leader!

Tribe leaders must write and speak

Generalized Reciprocity is investing energy or resources in your people without an immediate return.

What is a specific, altruistic form of this investment of favor or support you can make in one of the important members of your tribe?

_____
_____
_____

Who is that person and why do you choose them to give your limited resources to?

_____
_____
_____

Balanced Reciprocity is an immediate return of energy you can give to reinforce honorable behavior to someone in your tribe

What is the specific behavior being rewarded?

_____
_____
_____

What is the immediate reward from you as Tribe Leader?

_____
_____
_____

Negative Reciprocity is the push back or uncomfortable response when a tribe member does something dishonorable such as crossing a clear boundary, behaving in a manner that is not in alignment with tribe values or not following through on a project.

What is a specific and recent example of this negative behavior?

_____
_____
_____

Who was the person and what is an example of effective Negative Reciprocity from you as Tribe Leader?

_____
_____
_____

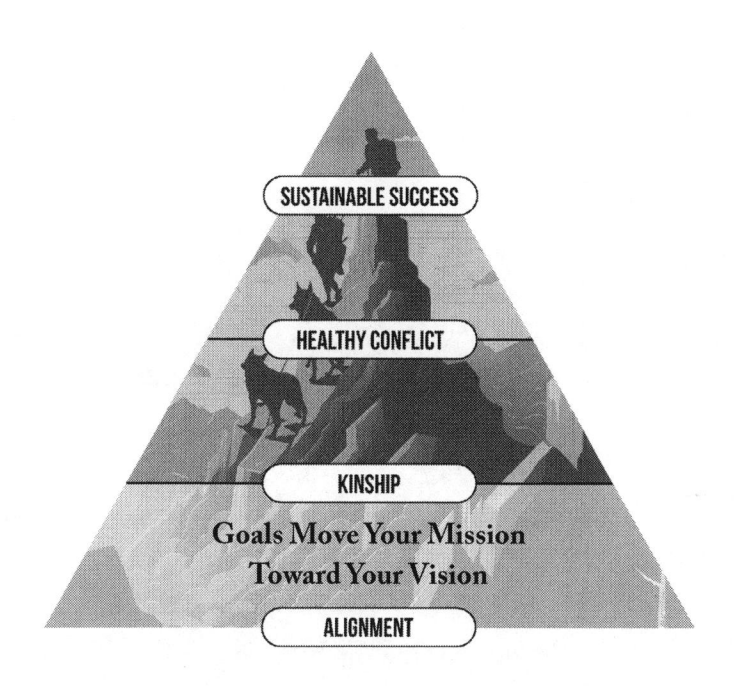

STEP 10 UP THE TRIBE TRIANGLE:

Goals Move Mission Toward Vision

Goal, *noun. The end toward which effort is directed.*

"Goals are dreams with work boots on."
–Dave Ramsey

Goals are how we look at our Tribe's shared, aspirational vision and ask ourselves what shape does this have to take to become real? **Goals are the roadmaps and deadlines we put on that shared vision.**

Remember the three Big Questions?
1. Where am I?
2. Where do I need to go next?
3. Who do I need to be to get there?

Goals are strategic ways to bridge what is with what could be. They answer the question, where we need to go next and also inform who do we need to be to get there? This process is inherently motivating for all members of your tribe. In addition, goals not only benefit from being shared (transparency) but also help drive transparency because they help clarify what people are working on, or need help with, that increases collaboration.

Goal setting is also vital for the morale and confidence of you and your team. Setting goals puts us in the driver's seat of our journey toward your tribe's shared vision which is inherently big and aspirational and can therefore be overwhelming. Goals help chunk this down to manageable size.

Vision big but work small

Ask yourself what single goal could you and your team accomplish that would have the biggest impact on your success and move you toward your vision? Once you have established this target it's time to make the steps clear, manageable and bite sized. That's the only way elephants get eaten.

There are many goal-setting systems and the most popular have acronyms. This makes them memorable and therefore practical and useful. Systems that are brilliant but not practical are impressive but not useful. Here are three practical and powerful goals setting systems. Modify these to fit your team and your culture or make your own!

- SMART
- PACT
- GRAILS

SMART Goals

SMART goals are probably the most well-known of the goal-setting acronyms.

- Specific
- Measurable
- Attainable (or accountable)
- Realistic
- Timebound

<u>Specific</u> is the detailed, well-defined and granular target you are committed to.

<u>Measurable</u> is a criterion and result that allows you to manage your progress and also a test of whether or not your goal is truly specific.

<u>Accountable.</u> We will always do more for others than we will do for ourselves. This is the secret core of honor-based heroism and it always comes from tribe. Get transparent, collaborative and reciprocal. Who are you transparently sharing this goal with?

<u>Realistic</u> is the vital question that defines whether a goal attainable or not. Unrealistic goals erode confidence and morale of you and your tribe.

<u>Timebound</u> is where the rubber meets the road. We need deadlines to create a sense of both urgency as well as movement.

PACT Goals

PACT goals are another variation that is commonly used in successful teams and organizations.

- Purposeful
- Attainable (or accountable)
- Consistent
- Trackable

Purposeful is alignment with vision. This is the significant, meaningful Big Game we hunt. Is the goal a step in the correct direction toward your Shared Vison?

Accountable. We will always do more for others than we will do for ourselves. This is the secret core of heroism and it always comes from tribe. Get transparent, collaborative and reciprocal. Who are you transparently sharing this goal with?

Consistency is king. Is this action continuous and repeatable? Can I build practices into rituals so this is ongoing and efficient? When will these consistent actions happen and where?

Trackable. More impactful that measurable is the question did I do it or not? Yes or no?

GRAILS Goals

GRAILS is the goal setting system from the international men's leadership community K4. For more information please visit K4men.com

- Goal
- Reason
- Allies
- Integration

- Learning
- Sacrifice

Goal is the specific, detailed and therefore measurable action you are committed to.

Reason is the motivation why you are inspired, engaged and committed to make that goal happen.

Allies are the people on your team that you will transparently share this goal with and who will collaborate with you and hold you accountable.

Integration is the regular and repeatable steps you will take to actually implement this goal. When and where will this action take place in your daily practice?

Learning is the new skill or behavior we will have to explore, discover and implement to make this new goal happen. If we could already do it we would have already done it.

Sacrifice is the thing we will have to give up making this new action or goal happen. Nothing is free and this goal is going to cost you things such as time, money, freedom and comfort. Name them so you can own them.

Notice, like everything else that we want to pull from the fog, goals must be written down and spoken for them to be clear and implemented and successful…

Tribe leaders must write and speak

What single goal could you and/or your team accomplish that would have the biggest impact on your success and move you toward your Shared Vision?

_____
_____
_____

Pick a goal-setting acronym from the list above and really fill it out. You will be surprised at how powerful the act of just answering and clarifying these questions is. Do it with your people.

_____
_____
_____

```
       SUSTAINABLE SUCCESS

        HEALTHY CONFLICT

            KINSHIP
    Brand is Not Your Logo
       it is Your Reputation
           ALIGNMENT
```

STEP 11 UP THE TRIBE TRIANGLE:

Your Brand is Not Your Logo it is Your Reputation

Steve Forbes said, "Your brand is the most important investment you can make in your business." This is profoundly true and the cost of that investment is the energy you put into the building and maintaining of your Tribe Triangle foundation of alignment. Ultimately, *your brand is what you do and how you do it.*

Your customers will never love a brand until your team loves it first

Brand is not just an appealing logo, color or a slogan (although these can be part of a brand). What your brand actually is, is your *reputation*. There are few things of more long-term importance than that. Your reputation determines your individual and tribe destiny as much as character and values.

> *"Branding is the art of aligning what you want people to think about your company with what people actually think about your company. And vice-versa."*
> *–Jay Baer*

A brand is a name or symbol that distinguishes your tribe and your tribe's products, services and possessions from others. The term 'brand' originated from the mark that is burned onto livestock to identify them from other cattle in the area. This was a practice used as far back as the ancient Egyptians over 5000 years ago and is still in use today. The term 'brand' has now expanded into a much larger context including identity and meaning.

Your brand is the banner that calls in your people, whether they be supporters, team members or clients. It is what they will rally around to conduct their lives. This is especially true for the hard and scary times when your people are threatened and uncertain about meaningful decisions.

The people attracted, then committed to your brand become members of your team or supporters of your team in the context of sports, causes and commerce. This is a function of *affiliation* and is a powerful driver of tribe and identity. Think of the times you have seen or worn the logo of a sports team, car or other product. Ferrari is considered the world's most powerful brand according to the Brand Finance organization. Its reach is vastly larger than the people driving their cars because it represents the three pillars of the Tribe Triangle foundation. What does the Ferrari brand say about an aspirational lifestyle vision, a set of clear values and a mission to work towards?

Brand is an act of visually proclaiming what you stand *for* and who you stand *with*.

People do business with other people (and organizations) they *know, like and trust*. Branding is the intentional act and art of becoming known, likeable and trustable.

Brand contains all the 3 components of your foundation of alignment.

- Vision, what aspirational experience or future do you stand for?
- Values, what is your creed or slogan that dictates your code?
- Mission, what do you actually do and how you do it?

3 types of brands: **company, product and personal.**

Company brand

Every successful organization has a brand. This is true for every company you can think of from McDonalds to the US Marines. Brand is a symbolic form of sharing complex information in a concise visual way. Think of how long it would take to explain the lifestyle vision, values and history of Ferrari? All that can be done in 1 second when you see that black stallion on that yellow shield.

The Ferrari logo is literally a coat of arms for the Ferrari brand. Not long ago, every family also had a brand such as a coat of arms that contained all the relevant information that company brands do now.

Even the slogan that is a universal part of a brand or ad campaign had its origin in ancient family crests which included a motto which was a short aspirational phrase that represented the family.

The motto of the US Marines is 'Semper Fi' which means 'Always Faithful' in Latin. Most of the organizational brands you can think of also have mottos, slogans or catch phrases. This short phrase can be a powerful addition to your company or family brand because it can convey your why, how and what in a more literal way than just a symbol.

Product or Service Brand

This is the individual product or service within a larger company brand. It is specific to that unique product or service but still part of the whole. Sometimes this is done by repurposing a well-known font (think Coca-Cola) or graphic (think of the hundreds of different versions of the Ferrari logo on different model cars or clothes). Again, regardless of the different versions of your brand across various products or departments they will all eventually meet the test of *is the customer happy?*

"You can't build a reputation on what you are going to do."
–Henry Ford

Personal brand

You have a personal brand already, it just may not be intentional and defined. Remember, brand is reputation and your personal brand is the reputation of *you*. **Your brand is what other people think about you *when* they think about you.**

1. What do you wear and how do you look?
2. How do you speak and write?
3. How do you act and what are your actual core values that drive

those actions?

Brand is the reputation of your organization or family. Regardless of how aspirational, visually pleasing and well-intentioned your brand may be, it will eventually come to represent and symbolize *what you do and how you do it*. Your behavior will literally create the value of your brand in the same way it creates your destiny.

How you establish and maintain your Tribe Triangle foundation of alignment is an act of branding at the highest level.

Tribe leaders must write and speak

Ask 3 powerful allies you have what 3 words they would use when they think about you or talk about you to others. Ask for one of these words to be critical!

_____
_____
_____

What is your Power Outfit that you feel the best in?

_____
_____
_____

What is a short phrase or motto that embodies the energy of your family or team's vision, values and mission?

_____
_____
_____

SUSTAINABLE SUCCESS

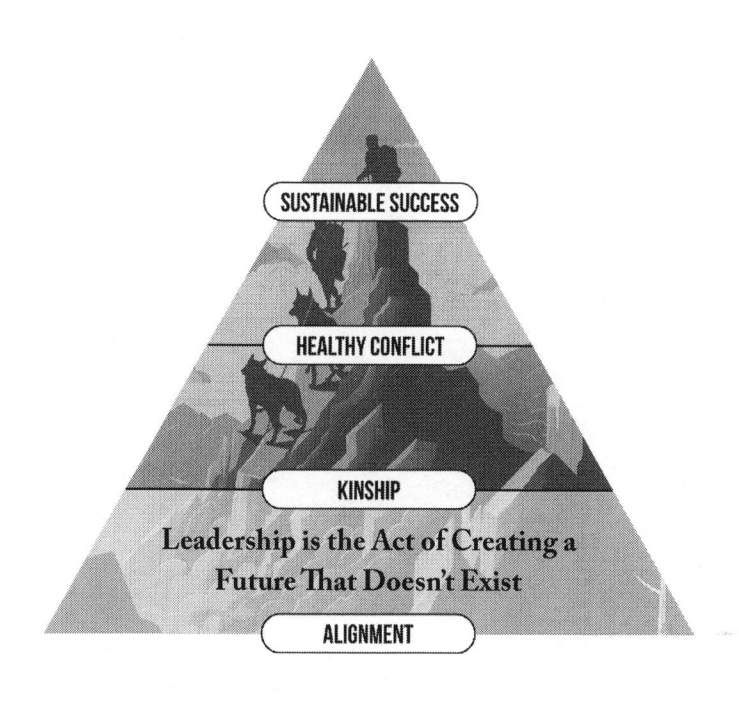

HEALTHY CONFLICT

KINSHIP

Leadership is the Act of Creating a Future That Doesn't Exist

ALIGNMENT

STEP 12 UP THE TRIBE TRIANGLE:

Leadership is the Act of Creating a Future that Doesn't Currently Exist

lead·er·ship
/ˈlēdərˌSHip/

noun

The action of leading a group of people or organization.

"*Leadership is action not position.*"
–Donald McGannon

Leadership is the beating heart of culture and regardless of your title in the org chart or your current job description, you are the head of culture before you are anything else. What you DO literally creates culture because culture is simply the collective beliefs and behaviors of your people. Your kids aren't listening to you, they are *watching you*. The same is true for your employees, co-workers, clients and bosses. **You are what you do not what you say.**

This reality places leadership development as the primary function and source of creating and maintaining your Tribe Triangle foundation of alignment. Numerous studies have shown that on average most people are promoted into leadership positions in their early 30s but don't receive any formal leadership training until their early 40's. This leads to a 10-year, steep and bumpy learning curve of on-the-job training that leaves a wake of collateral damage and debris on both your people and projects.

There are many forms and styles of leadership but all of them start with self-leadership. This is where all leadership begins and ends. **You can only take a team, family or organization as far as you yourself have gone.** Let's take another step on that ongoing journey now!

Firstly, there is a fundamental difference between leaders and managers. Both are vital to the ongoing success of your tribe and you may be forced to play both these roles often at the same time. Understanding this distinction will be key to your people and project success.

Leaders are people who can see and create an aspirational future that does not currently exist. This is why vision, inspiration and innovation are such central core competencies of leaders. Remember, Napoleon called leaders "dealers in hope."

Managers are people who drive and maintain what *currently exists*. They put out fires and do the grinding work of implementing the heavy lift of keeping the wheels turning.

Both of these functions are indispensable for families and work teams. Because they are often roles that must be played by the same person (you) you must realize how and when to switch hats. Too much time visioning what could be and nothing gets done. Too much time spent in managing *what* is leads to lack of vitality and imminent decay.

How do we know when and where to play these two roles? A great exercise is a prioritization matrix or the Eisenhower box. This is a simple 2x2 grid with the two axes being *urgent* and *important*.

Remake this grid on a sheet of paper and put as many of your weekly activities as you can into the appropriate boxes. Do this with your tribe!

Leadership activities are in quadrant 2 (important but not urgent). *Management* activities are in quadrant 1 (urgent and important.) Activities in quadrant 3 (urgent but not as important) you should delegate if possible. Activities in quadrant 4 (not urgent and not important) you should kill. Killing unwanted behaviors and beliefs is both a leadership and management function and duty.

	Urgent	Not Urgent
Important	**Quadrant I** • Crisis • Pressing problems • Deadline driven projects	**Quadrant II** • Relationship building • Finding new opportunities • Long-term planning • Preventive activities • Personal growth • Recreation
Not Important	**Quadrant III** • Interruptions • Emails, calls, meetings • Popular activities • Proximate, pressing matters	**Quadrant IV** • Trivia, busy work • Time waster • Some calls and emails • Pleasant activities

You will notice that quadrant 3 which is the less important things that *you should be delegating* gets regularly pushed up to quadrant 1 after they become urgent. The ability to delegate these projects hinges on not only your ability to see and assign those duties, but also the ability of your team to understand and implement them.

This is another vital component to the leadership journey which is the fact that *the best leaders create other leaders.* Have you gathered and trained a group of people who are capable of managing?

- Do they understand and buy into the vision that you are all traveling towards?
- Do they understand and operate by your shared values so the decisions, actions and projects are done in alignment with those values?
- Do they practice the mission protocol of *transparency, collaboration and reciprocity* so you can confidently delegate missions to them?

Leadership development is the real-world implementation and application of psychology, philosophy, ethics and even anthropology (which is the study of humans). Leadership development is transforming and integrating the information of the world into practical wisdom *for the world.*

You deserve this journey.
Your people and projects demand it.

Tribe leaders must write and speak

Are you optimistically holding and sharing your *VISION* for the future?

___
___
___

When was the last time you shared or reaffirmed your tribe's Shared Vision?

___
___
___

Who needs to hear it again this week?

___
___
___

Are your actions in alignment with your stated core *VALUES?*

___
___
___

When was one time you made a sacrifice to stay value-aligned?

___
___
___

When was one time you recently made an out-of-value-aligned action?

___

Are you conducting your *MISSION* in a shared manner?

___

Have you modeled transparency by sharing what you are working on this week?

___

Have you modeled transparency by asking for help with that mission this week?

___

What is one project that you can delegate to your people to manage that will liberate you to lead your team toward your shared vision?

___

SUSTAINABLE SUCCESS

HEALTHY CONFLICT

KINSHIP

**Change is Hard and Scary
so Know Your Enemy**

ALIGNMENT

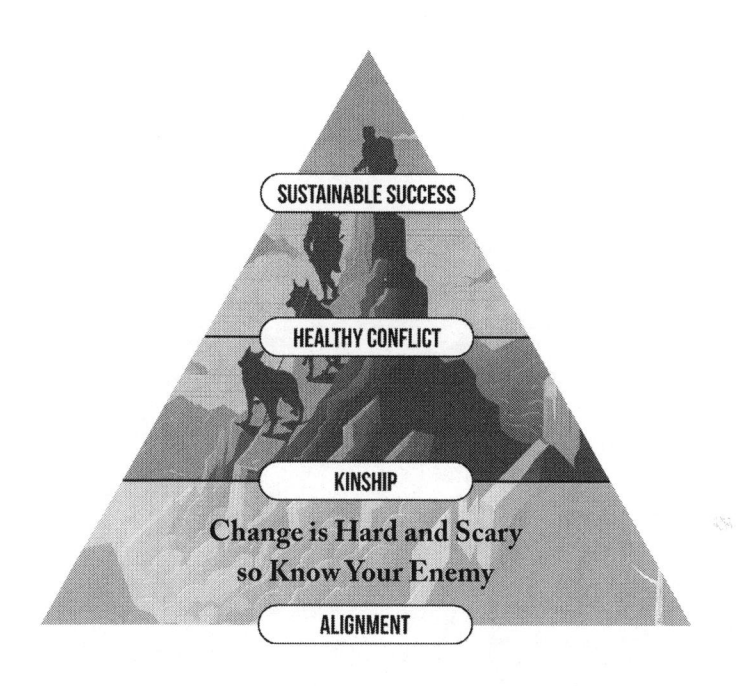

STEP 13 UP THE TRIBE TRIANGLE:

Change is Hard and Scary So Know Your Enemy

"The cave you fear to enter contains the treasure you seek."
–Joseph Campbell

Creating a foundation of alignment is a very steep and very challenging route up the culture creation mountain but it is the only way to get to the rarified air of *kinship*. Kinship is what unlocks the sustainable, significant performance and resiliency that all of us are questing after in our families and teams.

I have laid out these first 13 steps in a simple and sequenced roadmap but life is rarely like that. There will be resistance from your team and family because all these topics will trigger old stories and old coping mechanisms that protect us from being disappointed, embarrassed and hurt.

Most of the pushback you will receive, brave Tribe Leader, will not really be about you, per say. It will be about you being the scary and unwanted messenger of change.

Human history is filled with unkind treatment of messengers. Change agents are rarely well-received or well-accepted. Guard your heart and your authority during these times. Be patient but do not be paralyzed. You may need to fall back to safety but do not dig into old positions. Remember, it takes 30 days to establish a new habit, 90 days to create a new lifestyle (a collection of habits) and up to a year to enact sustainable change in a culture. This is the ongoing, arduous but exciting path we have chosen.

In addition to the resistance from your team, you will also undoubtedly discover ferocious resistance from yourself. Like your family and team, you also have a host of inner critics and self-limiting beliefs that this process will unleash like a floodlight carving through a cave of bats. Remember, these limiting beliefs are harmless and have no power except what you give them.

Also remember that you are the Head of Culture before you are anything else. What you DO literally creates culture in real time. What you DON'T do also creates culture. Experiencing this is to learn why the crown is so heavy. It is also why that crown is so powerful.

As Tribe Leader it is your duty to establish and model a *vision*, *values* and *mission* that are both powerful and public. This will also entail your transparent ownership of when you fail at living in alignment with that vision, values and mission. This intentional vulnerability and recommitment will establish that norm for your people. Below are the 3 best practices for implementing and maintaining sustainable change.

1. Develop awareness of self

Leadership is the act of making decisions that affect other people and this is why leaders are the head of culture. As a leader, your decisions are force multipliers in culture creation. Your decisions really matter so you need to get very intentional and very *skillful* at *how*, *why* and *when* you make your decisions.

The entire alignment foundation is based on *intentional choice*. This requires upgrading the decision-making process (which is why we spend two weeks on *values* which are the engine of decision making). The concept of intentionality is central to leadership because intentional ***choice is a product of awareness.***

Leaders must develop the ability to respond to situations instead of reacting to them. This ability to respond is literally *response-ability*

Keep developing your self-awareness because it is the foundation of response-ability, choice and the ultimate gift of free will. Read. Meditate. Find a coach. Join an accountability and growth organization.

- If you are a leader of people and interested in executive coaching to level up your own operating system in order so serve your team please reach out at philip@philipfolsom.com

- If you are a man interested in joining a pre-established honor-based culture to hold you accountable for your goals please reach out to K4mcn.com

2. Maintain vitality of self

Implementing and maintaining change is a long and arduous journey. Most of these growth-based quests never actually end and we must find a way to make them sustainable or risk burnout and quitting. Our people and projects demand us to maintain our vitality because as Head of Culture if we quit, they quit.

Take care of yourself. This does not mean binge or retreat. It means establish and stay committed to a lifestyle that augments your holistic vitality. I recommend that you look at 4 main vitality categories:

- **Career.** Is there some passion, creativity and positive feedback in your job? Is it fun at least for part of the day? How can you pivot your missions so they are better aligned to your personal vision and values so they will be more fulfilling?

- **Fitness.** How's your diet? How's your exercise regimen? Are you getting out to nature sometime every day even briefly?

- **Spiritual practice.** Do you pray, journal, meditate? Faith is the antidote to fear so find something you believe in that is bigger than yourself.

- **Relationships and community.** Do you have a relationship or community in which you have a tangible sense of belonging? Can you be vulnerable there?

3. Understand the behavioral change sequence in self and others

Much like the 4 levels up the Tribe Triangle, there are four main stages of behavior awareness and change. Understanding these phases will give you some confidence and, hopefully, patience with yourself and your team. Change is hard. If it wasn't, us leaders would be without a purpose!

The four stages of behavioral change begin with habits which become *practices* then *rituals* then *traditions*. Traditions eventually become old habits and the cycle begins again. Below is an expansion of these 4 stages.

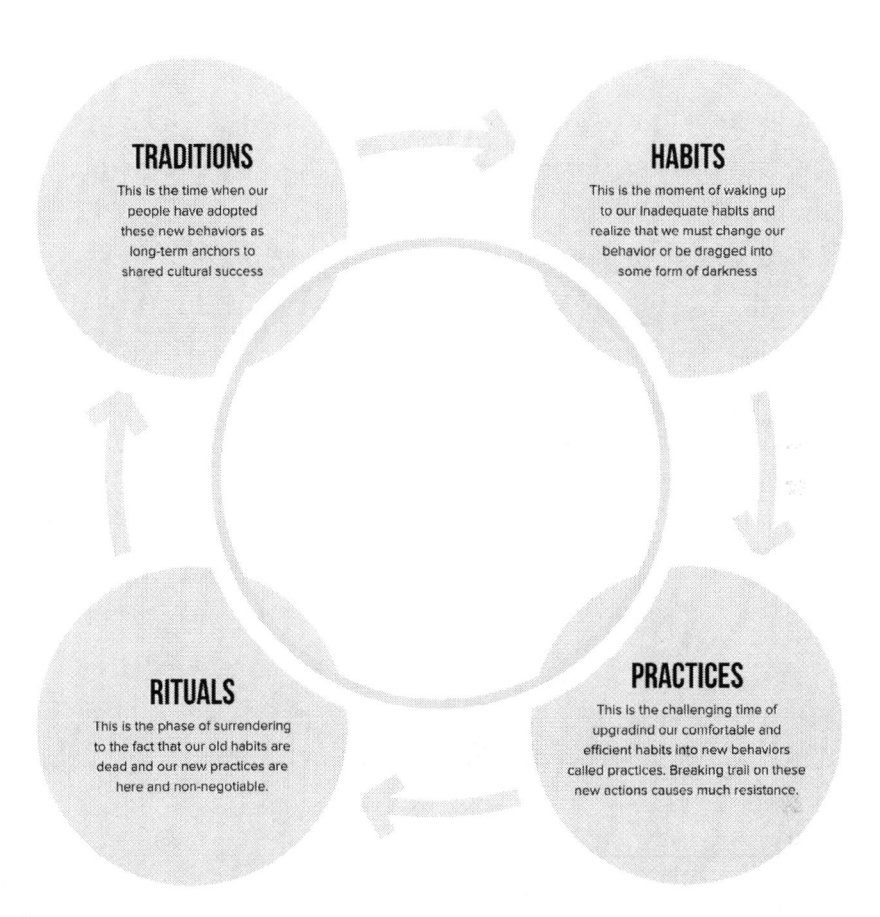

TRADITIONS
This is the time when our people have adopted these new behaviors as long-term anchors to shared cultural success

HABITS
This is the moment of waking up to our inadequate habits and realize that we must change our behavior or be dragged into some form of darkness

RITUALS
This is the phase of surrendering to the fact that our old habits are dead and our new practices are here and non-negotiable.

PRACTICES
This is the challenging time of upgradind our comfortable and efficient habits into new behaviors called practices. Breaking trail on these new actions causes much resistance.

Habits

We start with habits because they are the behaviors that we enact without thinking. This is the most efficient process available (which is why they exist). Habits operate at the base animal level of our consciousness and they are not designed for growth, only efficiency. To upgrade our habits, we must first wake up to the fact that our life is composed of habits.

Habits are the simple bricks that we build the cathedral of our life with. Are they mud or polished marble?

An example of this is to cross your arms in front of you. Notice the arm on top and also notice that this was not a choice but a habit. Now uncross your arms and recross them with the other arm on top. This was a choice. Also notice what you are feeling with the other arm on top. Uncomfortable, awkward and filled with resistance. You have probably quickly uncrossed your arms and you did it because that discomfort was inefficient and therefore uncomfortable which is universally avoided by all living things.

No one walks uphill unless there is a powerful reason. It is the same with change. The powerful reason for change is the journey of transforming your pride-based culture to your new honor-based culture. When you are forced to address old habits, you will begin to explore new and upgraded behaviors. This is when your old habits become new practices.

Practices

"Best practices usually aren't."
-Christopher Locke

Installing the new behaviors of practices is the source of the resistance that will come from both you and your team. Practices are always hard. This is because they are new and therefore energetically inefficient and new behaviors usually take more than 90% extra energy than our old habits. Practices are also hard psychologically because we are always bad at things we first start. Establishing and maintaining these new practices is demanding and at some point, we get tired, distracted or discouraged and we quit.

To break through this process, we need the support of our allies. These allies support you and hold you accountable for maintaining your new practices and each time you recommit to these new, growth-based behaviors you chip away at your old culture and lay a brick in your new foundation. If your allies are strong enough and you are skillful enough at following this map you will eventually break through to the next phase, rituals.

Rituals

> *"Ritual is necessary for us to know anything."*
> *-Ken Kesey*

Rituals are behaviors (practices) that are no longer a struggle because we are no longer fighting against ourselves.

Ritual behaviors can only be created when we have surrendered our old habits. When we are able to redirect all the energy we spent resisting ourselves into growth and vitality there is great progress made.

Like the earlier behavioral phase of practices, maintaining rituals takes tremendous energy. However, because rituals are non-negotiable and committed, we no longer must fight to maintain them which means we are only expending energy on the task and not ourselves.

Traditions

> *"Tradition is an explanation for acting without thinking."*
> *-Grace McGarvie*

Traditions are behaviors that are so engrained in our being and tribe that not only do we do them without resistance but we do them without thinking. This is powerful but also dangerous. Traditions reinforce those honor-based behaviors and encode them in accepted norms that we can do without the struggle of thinking or choice. They become efficient. They become habits. The cycle begins again.

Tribe leaders must write and speak

After you are done with this valuable journey up the Tribe Triangle, what is the next book you will read that will level up your awareness?

_____

_____

_____

Do you have a team or community that holds you accountable for your self-development? Who are 3 of those brave people who would (and have) given you tough love feedback?

1. _____
2. _____
3. _____

What is one vitality practice that you need to recommit to? (career passion, physical vitality, spiritual practice or community)

_____

_____

_____

SUSTAINABLE SUCCESS

HEALTHY CONFLICT

Kinship

KINSHIP

ALIGNMENT

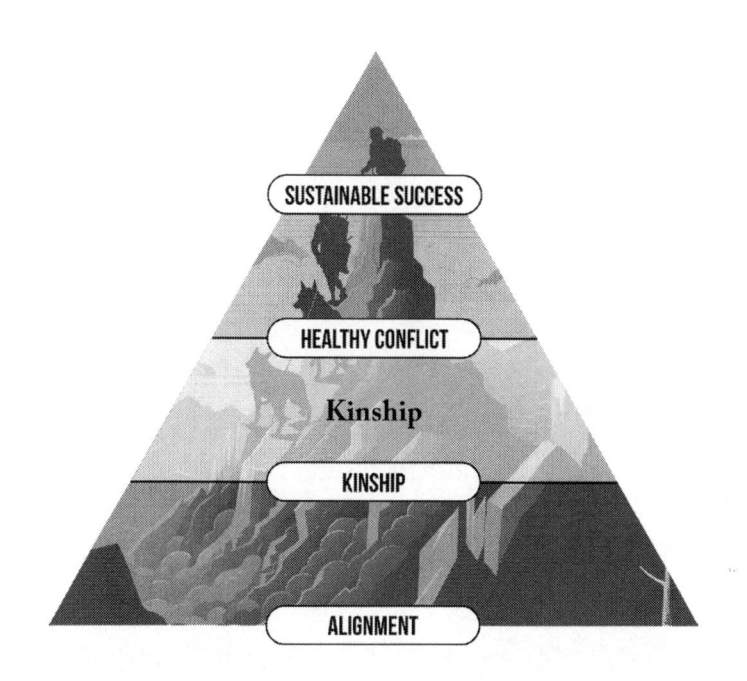

PHASE 2 UP THE TRIBE TRIANGLE:

Introduction to the Kinship Phase

Ubuntu is an ancient African word that means
"I am because we are and we are because I am."

Ubuntu is humanity.

If you have one of the culture foundation pillars of the Alignment level of the Tribe Triangle you have a group. This is vastly better than being alone or part of a random collection of lone wolves scavenging and fighting each other to get their individual needs met. If you have two of the culture pillars of Alignment you have a team. This is significant and enables you to survive in a challenging world. If you have all three culture pillars of Alignment, shared vision and mission, you have achieved the rare and powerful new level of an honor-based culture. You have created a tribe. This is the moment when the pack transcends the simple total of its members and becomes something significantly more effective, robust and resilient. This is the birth of kinship.

When we share a vision for the future, a common set of values that we operate by and our missions become collaborative and reciprocal it flips a psychological switch in the human brain and soul. We start to view each other as extensions of ourselves. We become part of something greater than the sum of its parts. This is the moment when co-workers become kin and will always look back as this team being the best team they were ever on.

Kinship contains the same root as the work *kind*. Kindness is the special behavior that we reserve for the people in our kinship system. We only go the extra yard, share resources and behave honorably and heroically in kinship systems.

All heroism in the history of humanity has come from kinship systems. Athletes will play injured for the sake of their team, mothers and fathers will sacrifice themselves for their children and soldiers will sacrifice themselves for their battle buddies. If you want to activate the greatness and meaning of heroism you will have to build a kinship system.

Kinship is also the source of resiliency, morale, deep friendships and the significance of service. Your journey toward freedom, meaning and sustainable success runs directly through, and from, your kinship system.

Take good notes on this process because like all systems they will tend toward entropy and your precious kinship system will be eroded by the pride-based world we live in and are surrounded by.

As Tribe Leader and head of culture, you will have to revisit and recommit to the relationship vitality and significance of kinship. It will prove to be the most important and meaningful resource on your journey and the longest-lasting component of your legacy.

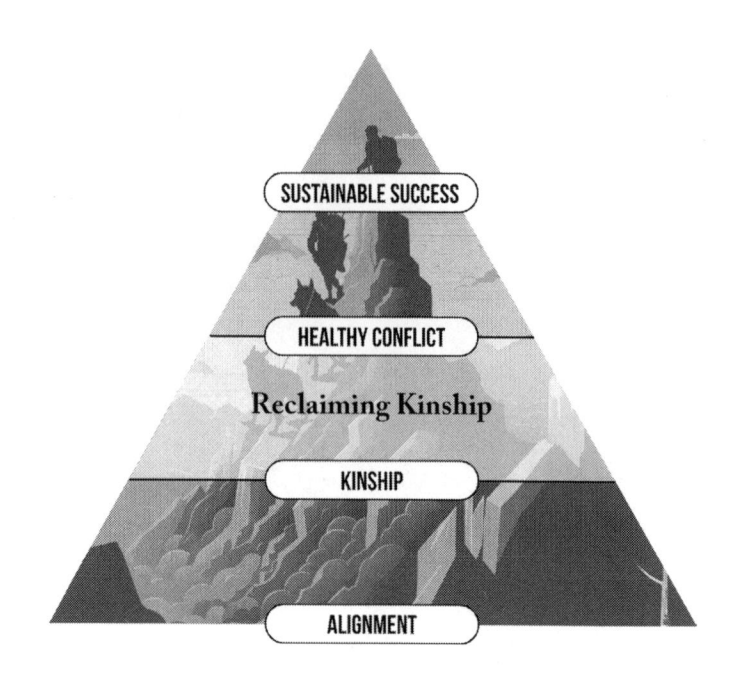

STEP 14 UP THE TRIBE TRIANGLE:

Reclaiming Kinship

"Society has a kinship-shaped hole in its heart."
−Philip Folsom

There are two Big Challenges that face your family and your work team, Tribe Leader. Fortunately, both of these challenges are resolved by the same solution and although that solution is very simple it can be very hard in today's society.

The first of these two Big Challenges is to discover the cause and the solution to our resiliency and mental health struggles. The second challenge is to discover the cause and solution to our physical and professional challenges.

The cause and solution to both of these Big Challenges is to acknowledge our lost kinship system that we are biologically and socially designed for and then reclaim it

We are going to do a deep dive into both kinship resiliency solutions as well as kinship sustainable success solutions in the next two steps. To do this we must first get a grasp of what kinship is and why it is such a vital component to humanity.

Humans need a tribe like a wolf needs a pack. Lone wolves do not thrive or experience resiliency and success. Neither do lone humans. We are built for the honor-based culture of tribe to the extent that both a lone wolf and a lone human are contradictions in terms. Kinship is the heart of tribe in the same way that reciprocity is the heart of kinship.

Kinship is a deep form of relationship experienced by people who share an affiliation in the same honor-based culture.

For literally hundreds of thousands of years that our species has been on the planet (and the 6 million years that our genus left the trees to walk the savannah of ancient Africa) we have lived in tribal organizations running a kinship-based operating system. This is corroborated by the anthropological research on every indigenous tribe from every era and every area of the world. Our default operating system is tribe and tribe means kinship.

Indigenous people do not have to answer the question of what the meaning of life is. It's simple: serve the tribe and receive honor, purpose and meaning by doing so. Without tribe and the inherent kinship system within it, we are stripped of the innate sense of meaning in life.

Similarly, indigenous people do not struggle with the misery of anxiety, depression, addiction and suicide that is currently accepted as a normal part of life by modern society. Indigenous people also do not suffer from the stress-induced diseases that are the top killers of people in modern society. This is all a function of intact kinship systems.

How do we cooperate successfully in a society where there are no traditional reciprocity kinship systems left? Artificial times require artificial means. We must create new kinship systems and these must be implemented strategically in the very center of our lives where they make the most impact.

With whom do you spend most of your time every day? For most people it is no longer our family, it is *co-workers at our jobs. This simple and unavoidable fact places these co-workers at the very center of our lives.*

Like it or not, your co-workers are some of the most important people in your life simply because you spend the lion's share of your waking hours with them. If you do not share deep and meaningful alignment with these people you will not have deep and meaningful experiences with them and therefor in your life. Reflect deeply on this.

I regularly hear people say 'those are *just* my co-workers' about the people they spend their lives with and that is a mental, emotional and spiritual disaster for humanity. Whatever you are doing with the majority of your time must generate meaning.

Whomever you are doing that with must generate a sense of belonging and reciprocity. Kinship is the key to unlocking the sustainable resiliency and success of this new framing of work and co-workers.

'Kin' is the root of the word 'kindness' and refers to the special treatment we reserve for people in our kinship system or tribe. If you want more kindness in your family, work team and community, create more kinship.

Tribe leaders must write and speak

Who are the three people you spend the most time with on most days?

1. _____
2. _____
3. _____

Using the techniques from the previous 13 steps of creating the alignment of kinship, what is one way you can deepen your relationship with each of those people from co-worker to tribesmember? (Shared vision, shared values, transparency etc.

_____
_____
_____

SUSTAINABLE SUCCESS

HEALTHY CONFLICT

Kinship Solutions To Resiliency Challenges

KINSHIP

ALIGNMENT

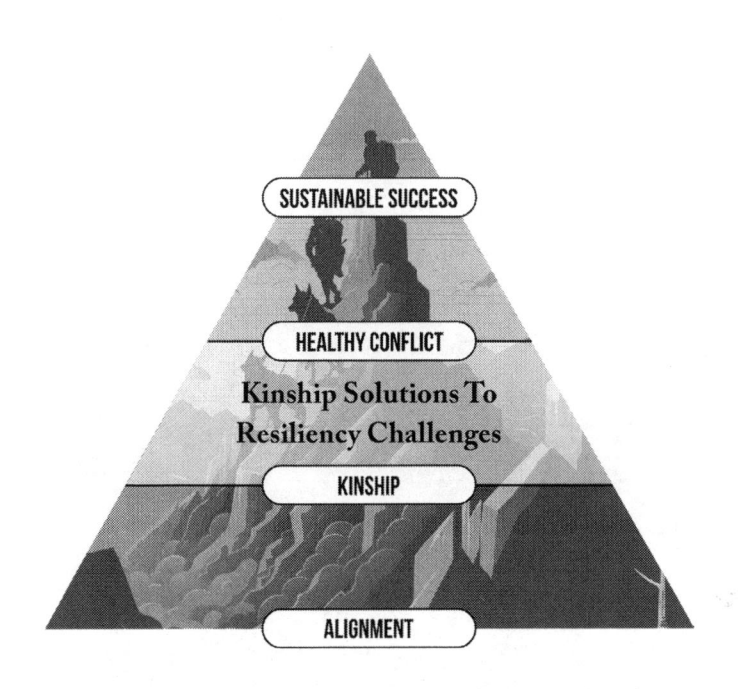

STEP 15 UP THE TRIBE TRIANGLE:

Kinship Solutions to Resiliency Challenges

Resiliency

(n.) The ability to become strong, healthy or successful again after something bad happens.

"Life doesn't get easier or more forgiving; we get stronger and more resilient."

– Dr Steve Maraboli

The factory setting and baseline emotional for humans is joy. When anthropologists first meet indigenous peoples, they report a very similar experience; we hear them before we see them because they are laughing and singing. Clinical anxiety does not exist in indigenous tribes who still maintain their kinship systems. Neither does clinical depression. Many indigenous tribes have no concept of what suicide is because it is such an inherently anti-human behavior.

We know in our bones that we have a core need for the connection of kinship. In fact, our need for *affiliation* is one of three most fundamental psychological drives along with autonomy and competence.

As we see the vital connection of kinship fading in almost every aspect of modern life, we can feel the dread and anxiety of isolation closing in. We find ourselves on social media platforms instead of communities, desperately clamoring for the external validation of 'likes' from 'friends' who are do not actually like us and are not actually friends at all.

Back in 1985, Americans reported having an average of three 'close others' and by 2004 that number dropped to one. Today, over 25% of Americans report that they do not have a single person to share a vulnerable challenge with. From 2013 to 2016 major depression rose by a staggering 33% and the clinical anxiety, addiction and suicide rate is rising even higher and faster within the last 5 years.

The few remaining pillars of tribe, kinship and community such as the church and other social institutions are crumbling from neglect or being actively pulled down. Even the seemingly invulnerable bastion of non-negotiable community, the workplace, is now being threatened by remote work and artificial intelligence. When we have no authentic connection with our people at work, the isolation of humanity will be complete. Do not underestimate the power of community and kinship, Tribe Leader. Rage against the dying of the light of kinship!

The effects of isolation are massive for both our psychological and physical quality of life. In a recent large-scale study by Professor Christine Porath, it was discovered that over 65% of people don't feel any sense of community at work and another study discovered that over 75% of people find it difficult or impossible to make connections with co-workers. Overall, the majority of workers in America feel physically and emotionally isolated at their jobs and report feelings of loneliness.

This sense of isolation has a direct impact on our physical and psychological resiliency and people who report a sense of belonging and thriving at work experience fewer feelings of burn out, miss less work and have significantly fewer doctor visits. This translates into substantial health care savings and more productivity for the organization. Stress and stress-related illnesses are the number one killer of people in western culture and the negative health effects of loneliness are equal to the impact of smoking 15 cigarettes per day. Most of this stress is simply a downstream symptom of lacking the core human need of *belonging*. Genuine belonging is a function of kinship.

Ironically, the experience of isolation today is happening while being surrounded and connected to more people than in any time in human history. What is lacking is the ancient need for authentic kinship with these people. Feelings of loneliness are so destructive to us because we are a species that is designed for community to not only thrive but to survive. Isolation (such as excommunication and banishment) in communal species is a brutal and slow death sentence. The fact that we would choose isolation over community is evidence of the toxicity of our current culture and how far we have strayed from our cultural factory setting of kinship.

Being a leadership consultant for the last 30 years I have gotten to work with a who's-who of notable companies and I can authoritatively say that joy is not the baseline for people working in corporate America. Tragically, it seems just the opposite.

Clinical anxiety, depression and suicide are all increasing at alarming rates. The clinical psychiatrist, Jordan Peterson says "if you have to face a dragon you should go to its lair or it will come to your village." The mental health dragon that we all knew was out there hunting our veterans and police has jumped the fire lines and is now in our village hunting in our corporations, families and schools. It's time to pull out the big guns of resiliency and the biggest one we have is reclaiming *belonging* which is the number one driver of resiliency.

We are inherently social creatures forced into a self-reliant world. We are built for kinship-culture and forced into career-culture. Authentic feelings of belonging are only found in families and organizations running kinship operating systems.

Creating kinship in your families, work teams and communities is the most important call to adventure you will ever receive, brave Tribe Leader. Reclaiming kingship is a steep and arduous road but we have the ancient, battle-tested roadmap of the Tribe Triangle to follow and you are enough. The call to kinship itself is your qualification.

Tribe leaders must write and speak

Who are 3 people in your tribe who would benefit from an authentic connection from you to increase their feelings of resiliency and belonging? When and how are you going to reconnect with them this week?

1. _____
2. _____
3. _____

SUSTAINABLE SUCCESS

HEALTHY CONFLICT

The Solution for Sustainable Success

KINSHIP

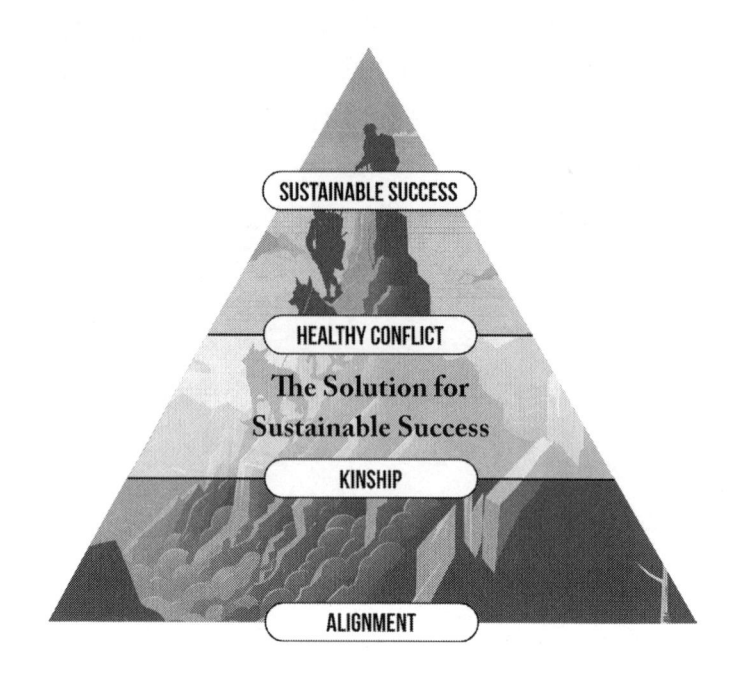

ALIGNMENT

STEP 16 UP THE TRIBE TRIANGLE:

Kinship is the Solution for Sustainable Success

*"If everyone is moving forward together,
then success takes care of itself."*
–Henry Ford

Significant success is a product of sustainable success. Success is not a sprint; it is a marathon. Consistency over time has been proven to drive the highest long-term results. Consistency cannot be maintained alone because we require the support and accountability of our team and tribe to pull us when we become distracted and our energy becomes diffused.

"If you want to go fast, go alone. If you want to go far, go together."
-African Proverb

Unfortunately, this collective shared journey is not shared by most American workers. Overall, most workers in America feel more physically and emotionally isolated at their jobs and report increasing feelings of loneliness.

This sense of isolation has a direct impact on job performance. Lonelier workers receive fewer promotions and report lower job satisfaction. Workers experiencing feelings of isolation in the workplace have less commitment and engagement. US Surgeon General Murphy stated *"At work, loneliness reduces task performance, limits creativity and impairs other aspects of executive function such as reasoning and decision making. For our health and our work, it is imperative that we address the loneliness epidemic quickly."*

Loneliness is the feeling we are left with when we lose the kinship level of our Tribe Triangle. If you are committed to bringing more sustainable success into your family, work team and community then you must address the rising rate of loneliness that is happening all around us.

In her large-scale research across multiple industries, Professor Christine Porath discovered that when people have deep connections and feelings of community at work, they are 74% more engaged with their jobs. In addition, they have a whopping 81% more commitment to the organization they feel kinship with. Overall, workers in kinship systems had a trackable 16% increase in overall job performance compared to workers who reported feeling isolated and lonely. Improving your company culture to kinship level is the best investment you can make to increase your competitive advantage.

According to Dr. Porath's studies, leaders who encourage employees to work in sustainable ways and model this sustainable behavior themselves create 55% more engagement and 53% more focus and substantially increased commitment to their projects and people. Tribe leaders truly are the Head of Culture before they are anything else.

To build a culture capable of sustainable success requires the creation and maintenance of kinship in our culture. **Investment in this level of culture upgrade creates eight times the return of investment in upgrading either strategy or technology.** This is one of the many reasons that in the leadership development space they refer to culture as king because it moves all the levers of sustainable success.

We have already explored the stages that are required to build this culture of kinship in the previous 13 steps up the Tribe Triangle but it is valuable to reflect on how that foundation of alignment drives the sustainable success of kinship.

The first pillar of alignment that creates kinship is *Shared Vision*. Establishing this north star to navigate from drives the sustainable success of motivation, confidence and resiliency. A shared vision of an aspirational future is the number one driver of sustainable morale and purpose.

This vision must be inspiring and include a journey of significance. Hunting big game with a team drives engagement and fulfillment. People want to participate in significant projects that provide meaning in their life. We can only do this collaboratively, remember, lone wolves cannot hunt big game. Publicly recommit to this early and often.

The second pillar of alignment that creates kinship is *Shared Values*. This vital culture block drives the sustainable success of trust, belonging, efficiency and most importantly, a shared journey of belonging. Like everything else *you* must model these shared values in all your decisions.

The third pillar of alignment that creates kinship is **_Shared Mission._** This includes increased transparency that creates the cohesive drivers of fairness, engagement and trust. Transparency of shared mission then increases collaboration which boosts competitiveness and confidence. Increased collaboration boosts reciprocity, which is the engine of kinship. Celebrate transparently and struggle transparently.

Sustainable success is built into tribe and kinship culture. Success is not a finite goal with a finish line. It is an infinite goal that must never end. If success ends then we end. This is ancient wisdom that we would do well to remember and reclaim.

Tribe leaders must write and speak

Review your tribe and note 3 good people who seem disengaged or dissatisfied.

1. _____
2. _____
3. _____

Do they need a reminder of your aspirational shared vision of the future? Do they need a demonstration of your shared values from you? Have you communicated transparently with them recently?

_____

_____

_____

Make it so, Brave Tribe Leader!

SUSTAINABLE SUCCESS

HEALTHY CONFLICT

Kindness is a Function of Kinship

KINSHIP

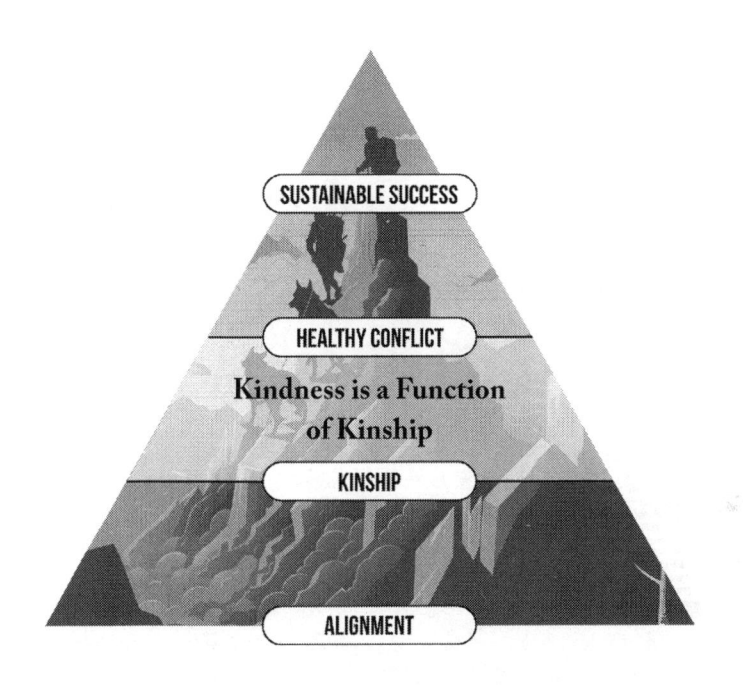

ALIGNMENT

STEP 17 UP THE TRIBE TRIANGLE:

Kindness is a Function of Kinship

"Kindness is the golden chain by which society is bound together."
–Johann Wolfgang Von Goethe

Kindness is the special behavior we reserve for our kin or the members of our tribe. Kindness is a special form of behavior that you simply cannot afford to give to everyone. We can always be nice to people but we cannot always be kind because kindness is going to cost you resources even if that resource is just stopping and saying hello. Try that in a busy place and notice you will not go anywhere or accomplish anything.

Who would you actually be compelled to stop and talk to on the street? Who would you cross the street to connect with or help? Who would you invite into your home and show hospitality to? Who would you help move? How many of your friends would help *you* move? We simply cannot do this for everyone in the world but we are *obligated* to do it for members of our tribe (or kinship system). This is one of the rules of kinship. There are responsibilities that come with being part of an honor-based culture and the most important responsibility is the duty we have to behave honorably to those within our tribe.

> *"Kinship and kindness share the same root of 'kin'. Kindness is the special behavior we reserve for our kin or the members of our tribe. If you want more kindness at home and work, increase your level of kinship."*
> *–Philip Folsom*

In studies from Yale University, they concluded that kindness is inherent to human beings along with altruism and empathy. This is based on the fact that kinship culture is our core operating system as a species. Without kinship we lose the crown jewels of humanity which are our empathy, altruism and kindness.

Although kindness is an inherent trait of humanity it is often trained out of us by the overly individualistic and competitive culture that is now the standard operating system of the modern world. All of us born into our pride-based world have learned to survive by taking care of ourselves first. This is the game we must all learn to play to be relevant and competitive today. Kindness will always require a short-term cost of our time and resources and we need to have the kindness operating system reinstalled to regain the long-term benefits of kindness. Kindness now must be taught and the best way to teach behavior, Tribe Leader, is to model it. Kindness is power.

> *"Human kindness has never weakened the stamina or softened the fiber of a free people."*
> *-Franklin D Roosevelt*

Cultures that contain kindness are proven to increase the resiliency and sustainable success of the organization. Kindness improves people's sense of well-being, mental and emotional health and even longevity. In addition, cultures that include feelings of kindness are substantially more competitive in the long run based on increased member engagement, retention and risk-taking.

Modeling kindness is a form of generosity that is returned in kinship cultures. This is the very definition of reciprocity. When we share kindness we get to share the happiness of those we are kind to.

One of the unattainable holy grails of modern organizations is to create a culture that is safe enough that people will actually ask for help. Unfortunately, this has been proven to be a pipe dream in individualistic cultures like the one we are living in. It is often too risky and vulnerable both interpersonally and intrapersonally for people to adopt the norms of asking for help. People simply do not regularly attend office hours in colleges and they do not often take advantage of well-meaning 'open door' policies that managers establish to be kind.

In our pride-based world we will never be able to create a culture of reaching out but we can create a culture of *reaching* in when we see a member of our family, team or tribe struggling. This is the greatest example of kindness we have and it is not only a form of human behavioral wisdom, but also the height of applied philosophy and leadership.

Ultimately, Tribe Leader, the start of sustainable kindness starts with kindness to ourselves. What we practice will be modeled. Kindness is intentional generosity not martyrdom. Make sure you put that kindness oxygen mask on first.

Tribe leaders must write and speak

Who reaches out to you when you are struggling? That is kindness and that person is kin.

_____

_____

_____

Who do you see struggling in your family or team now? Reach out and connect. It may benefit you more than them.

_____

_____

_____

SUSTAINABLE SUCCESS

HEALTHY CONFLICT

The Secret Power
of Altruism

KINSHIP

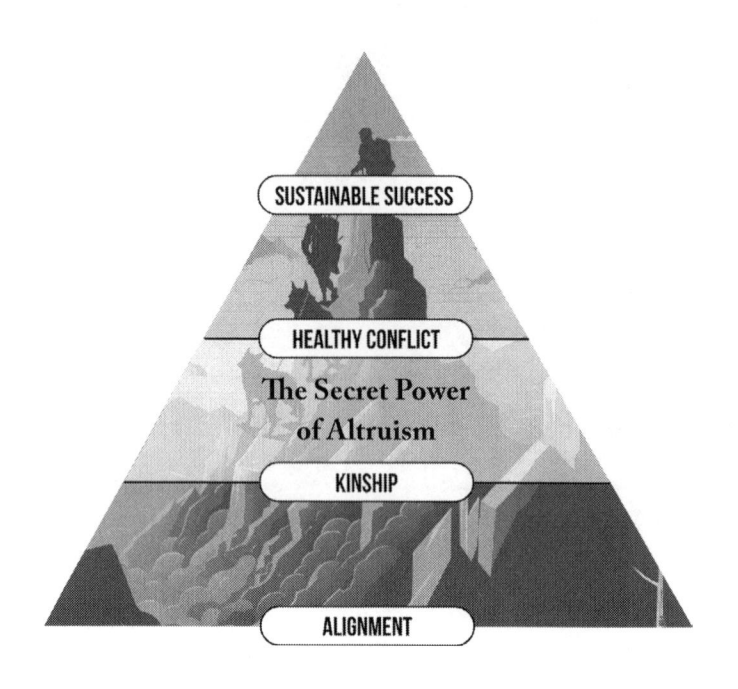

ALIGNMENT

STEP 18 UP THE TRIBE TRIANGLE:

The Secret Power of Altruism

*"Every man must decide whether he will walk
in the light of creative altruism or in the darkness
of destructive selfishness."*
–Martin Luther King

In the natural world, altruism is defined as behavior that benefits another at its own expense. For example, giving your food away to a hungry person at the cost of going hungry yourself. You can see how this uniquely moral and ethical behavior can only sustainably work in a kinship system because if that hungry person you gave your lunch to is in your tribe there is a good chance for eventual reciprocity whereas giving our lunch to strangers leads to our inevitable starvation. Again, we can be nice to everyone but cannot afford to be *kind* to everyone if it cost us our survival.

The difference between kindness and altruism is that kindness involves agreeable behavior that is driven by an obligation to a member of your tribe and altruism is driven by a belief of being selfless in the service of others. Altruism is the next level of kindness.

Altruism is not just moral, it is necessary to many communal species, however there are only a few species that display legitimate altruism. Selflessness may be innate to many communal species but it is not instinctual and must be taught. Actions that benefit the whole but compromise the one providing the action are altruistic and only a few advanced species display that. Wolves and humans are two of these species.

The famous anthropologist, Margaret Mead, was once asked what the earliest evidence of human culture was. Instead of the expected answer of 'stone tools, fire or pottery', she answered: "healed broken bones". Healed broken bones are direct evidence of the long-term commitment that interdependent species have with each other. To protect, provide and heal a member of your tribe or pack is going to cost you mobility, safety, opportunities and even freedom. Altruism is the cost of kinship.

The need for altruism is especially important for species that require advanced skill development to be successful, again, wolves and humans are examples of this and both species need substantial investment of resources before they are valuable members of the pack or tribe. Altruism is an evolutionary design feature that protects these valuable tribe assets. Protect your skill players, Tribe Leader!

Altruism is resiliency behavior because it provides the absolution of mistakes that are made

People make mistakes, especially when they are learning new skills. Altruism drives commitment to the tribe which increases long term payoff of skill investment. Altruism also maintains feelings of high morale and belonging because people who make mistakes will undoubtedly be forced to deal with shame and judgement. You cannot afford to deal with isolation in your tribe because the cost is engagement and you simply cannot afford to have a lack of engagement in your tribe. People live a long time, and it takes a long time for them to learn and develop into productive members of the tribe. This is as true now as it was in earlier times. If we don't take care of the developing members of our tribe and maintaining a culture of engagement we will be unable to thrive.

These feelings of well-being that come from altruism are also shared by those of us committed to selfless behavior and studies have shown a direct correlation between sacrificing for others and a sense of happiness and wellbeing.

Altruism is success behavior because it increases risk taking and competitiveness

The safety of altruism drives the resiliency that is required for risk-taking which is a vital function for a predatory species such as ourselves. This example of altruism is well demonstrated in our military ethos where we have strong commitments about not leaving any soldier behind even if it costs us massive resources to enact. Similarly, we do not shoot our wounded or even the wounded of our enemies even though the cost for this altruistic behavior is often substantial. The fact that soldiers understand that this altruism exists makes risk-taking much more palatable and this is another substantial form of resiliency and competitiveness.

Risks of altruism

Exhibiting altruism to everyone in the world leaves you depleted and unable to serve. You cannot pour from an empty cup, Tribe Leader, and you must put your oxygen mask on first for you to be able to serve those next to you. In addition, if we end up helping too much then we create enablement and eventually resentment. Don't cripple your people!

"Help someone, you earn a friend.
Help someone too much and you make an enemy."
-Erol Ozan

Altruism is the 'right thing to do' but it only functions in an ongoing way within an honor-based or kinship system. This is why we are exploring this powerful topic only after we have established our culture of alignment. There must be reciprocity and kinship established first, even if that reciprocity is so far out we cannot see it. The best time to plant a tree is 20 years ago and the next best time is now. As a species, we must keep planting trees that we will never personally sit in the shade of. Sometimes building an honor-based culture can feel like planting that tree. This is altruism.

Tribe leaders must write and speak

Who is a valuable member of your tribe who has made a recent mistake and would benefit from a healing absolution from you, Tribe Leader?

_____
_____
_____

Who is a valuable member of your tribe who has been wounded by a setback of some sort and would benefit from some compassion from you, Tribe Leader?

_____
_____
_____

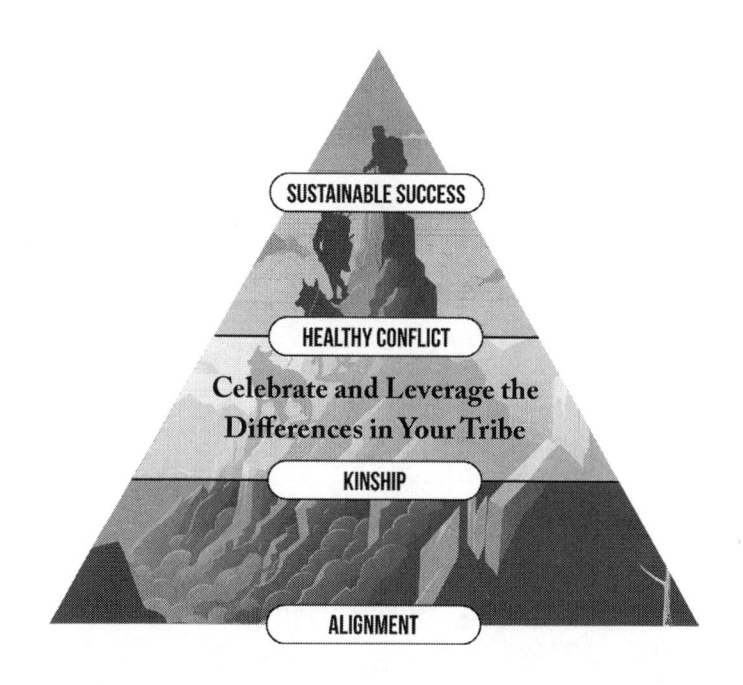

STEP 19 UP THE TRIBE TRIANGLE:

Celebrate and Leverage the Differences in Your Tribe

"Strength lies in differences not in similarities."
—Steven Covey

The differences within your tribe will be your competitive advantage or they will be your undoing. The sequence of moving from similarity to diversity is vital to make this work.

People gather and join on the basis of our similarities; however, we grow, develop and innovate on the basis of our differences. The order of this is vital. Alignment first, diversity second. If we are able to understand and implement this order, we reap the benefit of both the foundation of shared vision for the future, values that drive behavior and a collaboration of a common mission. in addition, we access all the power of innovation and versatility that diversity brings to teams. Think deeply on this, Tribe Leader.

An example of the power of differences is specialization on a team. Teams of skilled specialists will always defeat teams that consist of generalists. Again, this is only true when the team of specialists is aligned on a shared mission such as the shared winning of a team sport, hunt or mission.

American football typifies this form of specialization and even the players who throw, catch and kick the ball all wear pads and helmets. They all can run and tackle and are expected to. Wolfpacks also consist of specialized roles but they all bite. Military special forces units consist of deeply specialized soldiers but all refer to themselves as 'shooters'.

Regardless of position, all football players hit.

Regardless of role, all wolves bite.

Regardless of specialization, all soldiers shoot.

Affiliation first. Specialization second.

Differences without alignment drive us apart and can shatter a team and a family. Differences *with* alignment can elevate an average team or family into championship status.

Differences in conjunction with alignment accelerate us. Studies have shown that aligned teams with more diversity of age, ethnicity and gender tend to be more innovative and creative across time. There are many reasons for this including the power of different perspectives that drive diverse approaches to challenges and different skill sets that not only improve projects but also stack with other different skill sets to create brand new, innovative products and procedures.

In addition, the simple fact that a diverse range of people have access to a diverse range of information and personal experiences drives a more nuanced and collaborative world view and culture. Being embedded in multi-cultural environments with a shared mission tends to expand the process of personal reflection and expression. This is the forge of personal growth and development which always leads to increased resiliency and performance over time.

Differences in your team creates more opportunities for successful outreach by increasing rapport with clients. This form of marketing specialization can accelerate customer acquisition and also power customer service.

The ability of a Tribe Leader to establish a culture foundation that is so strong that it is able to take advantage and celebrate the diversity of humanity signals and models a commitment to collaboration and teamwork.

Tribe leaders must write and speak

Is there divisiveness in your team? What form of alignment do you need to reinforce so the differences become competitive advantages again?

_____

_____

_____

Is there diversity and specialization in your team that you are not taking advantage of to drive innovation?

_____

_____

_____

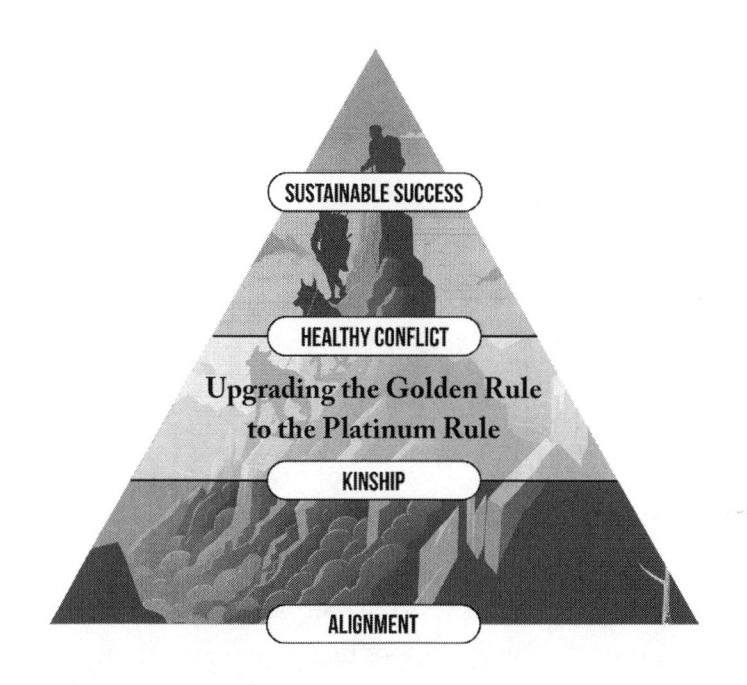

STEP 20 UP THE TRIBE TRIANGLE:

Upgrading from the Golden Rule to the Platinum Rule

"Treat others the way they want to be treated,
not the way you want to be treated."

Step 19 contained the potential power of accessing the differences that exist in your team. These differences are the raw ingredients that drive the human competitive advantage of adaptability. Step 19 also underscored the vital need for solidifying your team's foundation of alignment and similarity *before* you unleash their differences.

The transition from the universal Golden Rule to the rare and elite Platinum Rule follows this same sequence; you must establish your team's Golden Rules before you explore and implement the Platinum Rule.

Your people are unique. This is what makes them special and your team sustainably successful. Capitalizing on these differences in an intentional and strategic way is how you unlock and maintain this competitive advantage. This is the transition from the Golden Rule to the Platinum Rule. Implementing this cultural upgrade in your team will radically improve relationships of all sorts and lead to:
- Increased feelings of belonging, engagement and retention
- More authentic feedback, communication and accountability
- Improved conflict resolution and risk-taking
- Increased marketing awareness and sales

All modern societies have some version of the Golden Rule and it is embedded in the cultural norms of every modern culture. The concept dates back to at least Confucian times 500 years BCE and some version of the Golden Rule appears in all the major religions including Buddhism, Islam and Judaism and Christianity where is states in the bible, *"Do unto others as you would have them do unto you." (Matt. 7:12)*.

The Golden Rule is a designed for people who are not in a kinship system and who do not share the safety that is created by a common vision, values and mission. When dealing with people outside of our kinship systems we must step down into an impersonal set of behaviors that are intentionally superficial and universal.

We can witness and experience these shallow, guarded behaviors by becoming aware of the norms that operate in common areas such as banks, airports and elevators. Notice how people stand, act and speak. Notice how uncomfortable it *feels* in these places? That feeling is the human experience of being around strangers and it is deeply disturbing at a biochemical level. Cortisol, adrenaline and other stress hormones all spike when people engage with others outside of their kinship systems. The Golden Rule provides a baseline of shallow but safe behavior that enables stressed people to do business and live life in the presence of strangers.

The Golden Rule enables surviving but does not activate thriving. For that, we are going to have upgrade our operating system to the Platinum Rule.

The Golden Rule has been criticized for generations by philosophers and leaders who saw it as being valuable for a baseline for social behavior but limiting in the capacity for building intimacy, competitiveness and sustainable success. Both Friedrich Nietzsche and Immanuel Kant were the first to question the premise of the Golden Rule because in any relationship we can only know how *you* want to be treated and everyone has vastly different upbringings, belief systems, values and personal histories. How you want to be treated is bound to be different than everyone else you work with particularly with the people you work or live with on a regular basis.

To make these relationships work in more than superficial ways, we are going to have to dig deeper. How do the individuals on your team need to receive feedback, especially *critical feedback?* How do they engage with, and resolve, conflict? This pertains to your customers as well; how do they need to be marketed to and what are their priorities? These are all Platinum Rule questions and they pertain to your husband, wife, children and neighbors as well. This topic and these questions are some of the core competencies and challenges of leadership.

Finding out the wants and needs of all your close people can seem daunting, and it is. It is one of the reasons that honor-based, tribe cultures have a limited number of members before they collapse into larger, pride-based individual-centric communities. When that happens, the Golden Rule is resumed.

Understanding this, you can now see why all the big kinship upgrades in the Tribe Triangle can only happen when you have done your foundation work of building alignment!

The first step of upgrading to the Platinum Rule is to express your communication needs first. Remember, Tribe Leader, you are the head of culture before you are anything else and by modeling the specific ways *you* need to be critiqued, challenged and praised will empower others to express their individual needs as well.

Conducting an individual or group conversation of sharing these Platinum Rule needs is one of the most engaging and valuable exercises you can do with your family and work team. You deserve the Platinum Rule. Your People demand it.

Tribe leaders must write and speak

How do you best receive personal critical feedback? Private or public? Direct and immediate or in a more structured way with examples?

_____

_____

_____

When you get stressed out and overwhelmed how do you need to be supported? Challenged and acknowledged or nurtured and reassured?

_____

_____

_____

How do you need conflict to be engaged with and resolved?

_____

_____

_____

Ask these same questions (and any others that come up) to the members of your family and work team.

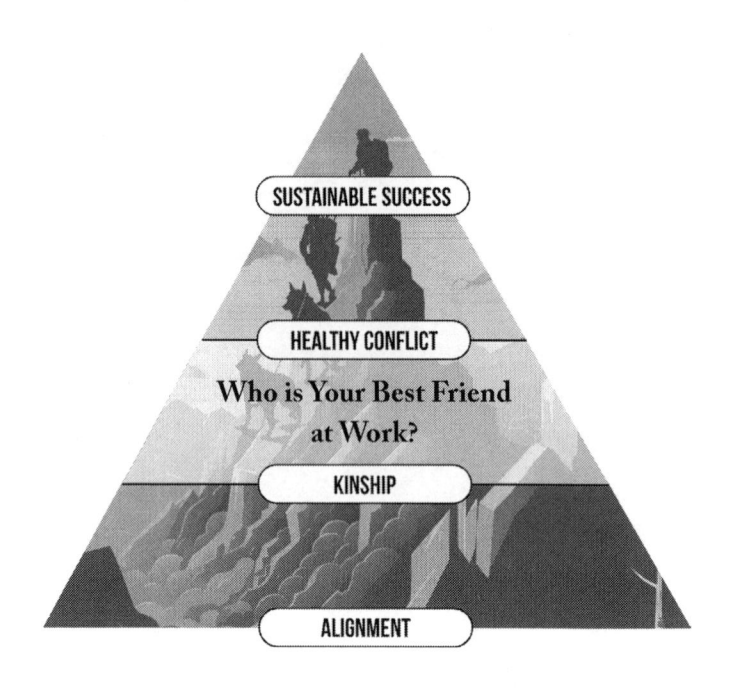

STEP 21 UP THE TRIBE TRIANGLE:

Who is Your Best Friend at Work?

"The people that you work with are, when you get down to it, your very best friends."
–Michael Scott

One of my mentors, Dr. Steven Johnson used to tell me that if you remove alcohol, sports and work, people in today's society don't have friends. He's right because all the other big friendship-generating community institutions such as the church, communities and fraternal organizations have faded in relevance and participation. Work is the last shared institutional source for meaning and belonging and it is particularly important because for most people it is the center of their lives.

The most important resource we have in our lives is time and unfortunately, we don't realize the importance of time until something threatens that resource in some way. No amount of *'Memento Mori'* quotes will wake you up like the experience of an important window in life closing.

With the knowledge that time is our most valuable resource, where are you spending most of it? For most people that place is work. That activity is the most important thing you do in your life by the simple fact that you spend most of your life doing it. That activity *is* your life for much *of* your life. To have a shot at really thriving at life we all better learn to make the most of work and that is what kinship is all about. Friendships sit at the very core of that.

Your coworkers are the people you spend most of that time with. Regardless of how you currently feel about them, they are some of the most important people in your life. If the relationships you have with those VIPs in your life are not meaningful, authentic and fun then you will be lacking meaning, authenticity and fun in your life.

Remember that time in your life when you used to have lots of deep friendships? For most people, those times were when we were in a structured environment with a shared foundation of culture alignment such as school, team sports or the military. These are all examples of honor-based cultures and they all generate authentic friendships. A big part of this is a shared mission which is a core pillar of all honor-based cultures. A friendship is synonymous with kinship.

Friendships prevent isolation and loneliness and give you a chance to offer needed companionship, as well. This is one of the most powerful ways of creating meaning in life. Friends also increase a sense of belonging and purpose. Increasing friendships has been shown to improve feelings of happiness, mental health and reduce stress.

Friendships also increase resiliency. A friend is someone who you can tell sensitive and vulnerable information to and they will protect it. A friend is someone who has your back and you have theirs. This is the honor of reciprocity and a central pillar of belonging.

"Friendship is born at that moment when one person says to another, 'What?! I thought I was the only one!'"
–C.S.Lewis

Authentic and ongoing friendships (like all kinship systems) require a shared mission. At their core, friendships are energy exchange systems and energy cannot travel through a vacuum. People need a medium through which the energy of their relationship can flow. This used to be the shared mission of school, sports or the military. Now it is work where people are desperately searching for meaning and belonging and that, too, is fading.

We need a best friend at work to be fully engaged and committed and only 20% of people report having a best friend in this central part of most people's lives. Gallup reports that over 65% of employees globally are disengaged and 20% are actively disengaged and toxic to the rest of the people and projects. Humans need friends to happy, healthy and high performing.

Unhealthy corporate culture operates under the premise that "You don't come to work to make friends, you come to make money. Friendships are unprofessional." I would propose that just the opposite is true. Work is now the last bastion of shared experience in modern culture and it must be about more than making money. Your work is your life because it is where you spend most of it. Make it worth it. Make your friends. You will even make more money for it…

"A man's friendships are one of the best measures of his worth."
　　　　　　　　　　–Charles Darwin

Tribe leaders must write and speak

Who is your best friend at work? Let them know. You'll be surprised at how impactful this conversation will be.

_____

_____

_____

Are there other people at work with friendship potential? What is one thing that you can do to facilitate that powerful level of relationship?

_____

_____

_____

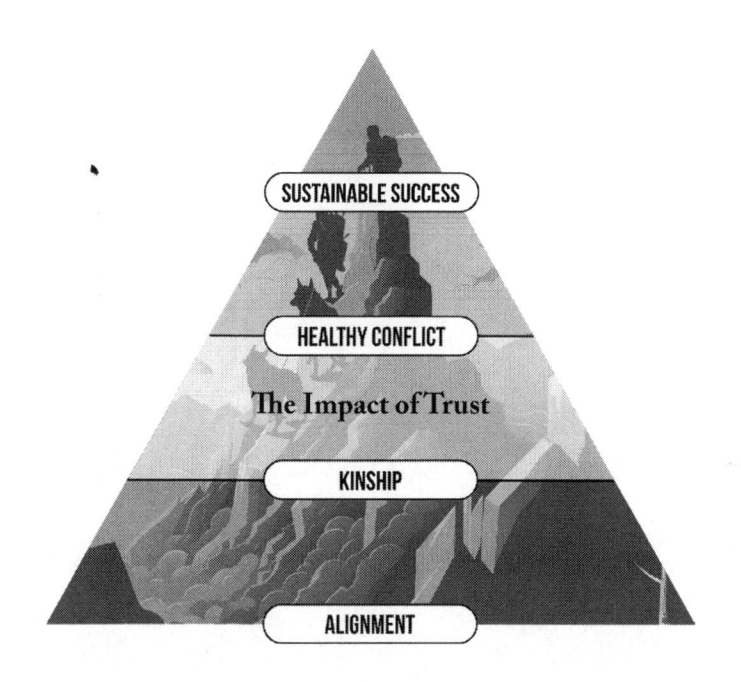

STEP 22 UP THE TRIBE TRIANGLE:

The Impact of Trust

"You must trust or life becomes impossible."
–Anton Cheko

Trust is a core ingredient of the kinship phase of your journey up the tribe Triangle. Like everything else in the kinship phase, it cannot be decreed or chosen and can only be achieved and earned by your hard, intentional work done during the alignment phase. Trust is a byproduct of your behavior while building alignment and can be described as behavior over time. Trust must be made and maintained.

Trust is behavior over time

Just as trust is a product of the foundation of *Alignment,* it also *serves* as the foundation of the next phase of the Tribe Triangle which is *Healthy Conflict.* We simply cannot sustainably and successfully engage with conflict without the foundation of trust and safety.

Trust-building is a byproduct of transparency and therefore can be a vulnerable experience. This is especially true during challenging times when you will need trust in your team more than ever.

People who work in high trust organizations report 74% less stress and experience 40% less burnout. In one study of over 1000 employees in high stress fields, 23% said they would work longer hours, offer more ideas (innovation) and would stay longer with an employer if they trusted their leaders.

Trust drives results and employees who trust their leaders exhibit 50% overall higher productivity at work especially in the categories of engagement, accountability, innovation and risk-taking. Trust is a legitimate and sustainable profit driver and 55% of business leaders report that a lack of trust in the workplace constitutes a legitimate foundational threat to their company.

Numerous studies from the **Great Place To Work Institute** and elsewhere have found that companies with high-trust cultures have greater financial success than those that don't. Unfortunately, trust is a rare commodity in today's society and only 20% of human resource leaders *believe their employees deeply trust company leaders,* and ironically, over 50% of employees report feeling that HR is trustworthy.

> *"If we don't trust each other, we are already defeated."*
> *–Allison Croggon*

Here are your marching orders, Tribe Leader. Firstly, to build trust you must first be trustworthy. Like everything else on this journey, you go first. You can instill trust in your team and family by trusting them first. This not only creates trust but also fosters a culture of accountability and autonomy (both of which begin to be seen in the next stage of the Tribe Triangle). Trust is behavior over time which means *consistency*. Your actions must coincide with your words and the intentions that you share. **Inconsistency will lessen trust.**

Secondly, listen more than you talk. Ask for feedback and act on it. Trust is the ability to be heard.

Lastly, invest in trust through transparent appreciation and recognition.
Over 90% of employees who receive thanks or recognition from their boss report feeling high levels of trust in that individual. This figure went down to 48 percent for workers who did not receive recognition. If you want to foster trust in your workplace, lean into the direct relationship between trust and recognition.

Like all the other steps during the kinship level of the Tribe Triangle, trust is vital for the quality at work now but is also necessary for the quantity of work that is available in the next phase of healthy conflict. Without trust we simply cannot explore and discover the power of workplace autonomy, ongoing accountability and self-directed, agile teams.

"Trust is the glue of life. It's the most essential ingredient in effective communication and the foundational principle that holds all relationships together."
–Stephen Covey

Tribe leaders must write and speak

Trust begins and ends with transparency and truth. To build trust we must first be trustworthy. What is a recent time that you have fallen short of your goals or standards and not transparently owned it to your people? When and how will you publicly own this uncomfortable share to build the trust?

_____
_____
_____

What do YOU need to trust your people? Have you ever shared that with them? If not, do so. If so, do so again!

_____
_____
_____

What do your people need for them to trust you? Have you ever asked them?

_____
_____
_____

SUSTAINABLE SUCCESS

HEALTHY CONFLICT

The Unexpected Power of Appreciation

KINSHIP

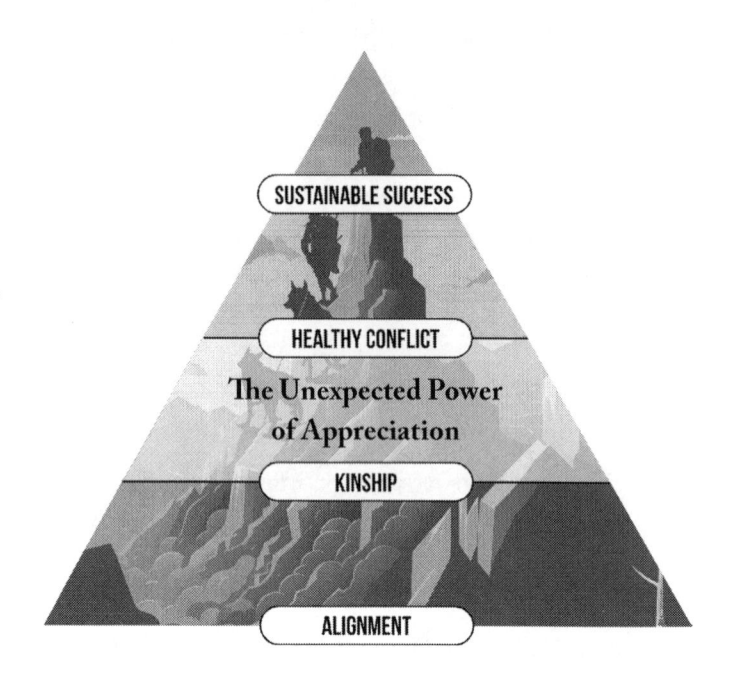

ALIGNMENT

STEP 23 UP THE TRIBE TRIANGLE:

The Unexpected Power of Appreciation

"The deepest principle of human nature is a craving to be appreciated."
–William James, American Psychologist and Philosopher

Appreciation is the glue that holds your tribe together and the gas in your kinship engine. It is the single highest driver of engagement and retention, according to a recent worldwide study and team members who feel like their leaders and managers are genuinely interested in their wellbeing and performance exhibit measurable and sustainable success. The same can be said for your family and community.

Over 80% of employees who are appreciated with some form of recognition in the last 30 days report being fulfilled at work. The **American Psychological Association** found that over 90% of employees who feel valued perform better and stay engaged at work.

In the Global Happiness Council's 2019 report there were clear correlations between appreciation, increased retention rates, and higher overall performance rating increases. This was particularly true for high-performing employees who received more frequent recognition.

The data in the study also revealed the powerful impact of practicing appreciation and gratitude on the givers themselves, and "The more employees offered praise, the more praise they received in return, creating a virtuous circle of positivity and success."

Unfortunately, like so many other vital aspects of kinship in contemporary culture, appreciation is in short supply and less than 40% of employees feel authentically acknowledged in their careers. According to McKinsey & Co., 52% of employees admit feeling undervalued by their managers. Employees who feel they are not recognized are over twice likely to quit as those who feel appreciated. Appreciation is fuel for the kinship fire of your team.

The current level of employee frustration and dissatisfaction underscores how critical it is that people in leadership positions make appreciation skills foundational to their organizational norms and practice it regularly.

Appreciation is a form of active respect and at the most basic level, appreciation makes us feel safe, which liberates us to do our best work. Without appreciation you will find that your team will struggle with risk-taking, innovation and accountability which are all aspects of the next level of the Tribe Triangle after kinship. Without appreciation you will struggle with maintaining kinship and you will not be able to move into the Healthy Conflict and Sustainable Success levels of your culture journey.

Next to physical survival, the greatest need of a human being is psychological survival—to be understood, to be validated, to be appreciated."
-William Covey, 7 Habits of Highly Effective People

There is a tendance to view and express appreciation as an aspect of our personal lives, however, appreciation in the workplace is especially critical because it satisfies the higher psychological need to feel a sense of belonging and meaning connected to something greater than ourselves in the place where we spend most of our time.

The desire for meaning at work is part of an organizational and psychological recalibration and return towards a more human workplace. When your people feel appreciated, valued and respected, you will see an organic movement of your tribe in the direction their fullest potential.

Like most of the other kinship drivers of society, appreciation skills are simply not utilized enough that they are normalized and comfortable. We have gotten rusty at using them. Like most other leadership tools and techniques, authentic expression is a perishable skill and one we can all get better at with practice. When you start building your gratitude and appreciation muscles, others will follow. Remember you are the Head of Culture before you are anything else!

Practice appreciation by starting with yourself
"A state of appreciation is one of the highest vibrational emotional states possible."
Jack Canfield, The Success Principles

If you have difficulty openly appreciating others, you will probably discover that you have some challenges appreciating yourself. Explore investing some time to ask yourself "What did I overcome today?" Give yourself the appreciation and grace that you would give to your people.

Studies show that by expressing gratitude, it raises your own happiness by as much as 25%. By sharing your appreciation for others, you will build and maintain healthier relationships, and will also feel better about yourself. This is another example of the reciprocity that is the engine of kinship and you are part of it!

One of the challenges of expressing appreciation is that it makes us vulnerable because authentic appreciation creates a powerful, human connection between both the giver and receiver. Letting people know that what they did benefited you and impacted you positively is an intimate act that elevates the relationship as well as performance. In the in depth 2019 Global Happiness and Well-Being Policy report the Global Happiness Council estimated that appreciation drives well-being and yields a 10% increase in productivity. This applies to you as well, Tribe Leader!

Appreciation is the act of giving recognition. When we recognize one another, it inspires the person we've thanked to pass that feeling on to someone else, leading to a ripple in happiness, well-being, morale, belonging and engagement. All these drivers of kinship directly improve profit, performance and productivity.

Be specific, timely and consistent with your appreciation
"Mankind will not die for lack of information;
it may perish for lack of appreciation."
-Rabbi Abraham Joshua Heschel, Who Is Man?

Having the awareness that appreciation is vital is the first step towards a culture of gratitude but the skills to deliver appreciation effectively and powerfully is where we get the real results.

The more specific you can be about what your vision is for the future and the values that will get you there the more effective your appreciation will be for your team. It will clarify what needs to be appreciated and help drive organization norms. When our appreciation is specific to the individual and specific to the behavior it carries genuine meaning.

In addition to specifics, we also must direct our appreciation at the intent and the effort not just the achievement. Acknowledge the stresses that were overcome and challenges that were faced above the project outcome. This is how we build kinship, trust and safety. These all supply the foundation for the accountability phase that comes next during the Healthy Conflict level of the Tribe Triangle.

Appreciation is a behavior incentive that you have a potentially unlimited amount of. It creates a wave of well-being and belonging that inspires and engages everyone it touches. The more appreciation is flowing in your tribe the more authentic human connections are being made as well as collaboration and active participation.

Appreciation is a self-driving engine. It powers and encourages successful behavior and the more success we create the more there is to appreciate. You deserve this. The success of your people and projects demand it.

Tribe leaders must write and speak

Review your top core, shared values and write them down.
1. _____
2. _____
3. _____

On your team, who is exhibiting any form of these behaviors and where are they doing it? Let them know! Private appreciation is more authentic and targeted, but public recognition and appreciation has a larger impact on culture as a whole. Repeated and consistent appreciation has a compounding effect of behavior and models the act of giving appreciation as a tribe norm.

_____
_____
_____

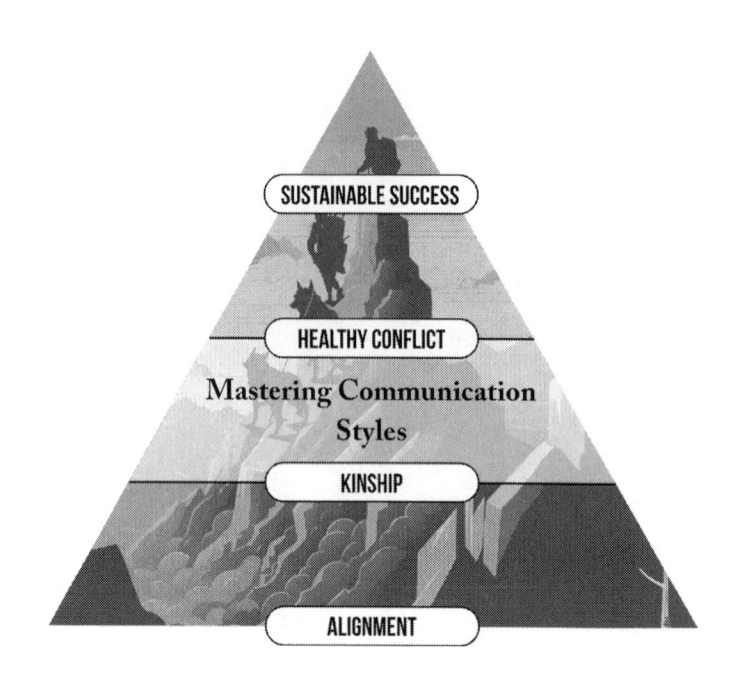

STEP 24 UP THE TRIBE TRIANGLE:

Mastering Communication Styles

"The art of communication is the language of leadership."
–James Humes

Communication sits at the very center of kinship. It is the lifeblood of relationships and the central driver of sustainable success. It is the crown jewel of all your kinship treasure and, like a diamond, your communication needs clarity in addition to being concise, correct, courteous and coherent.

Effective communication skills are the most important tools in your leadership tool kit. Developing the choice of what communication tool to use as well as the skill to use it is a lifelong process. Your communication skills will make and maintain the level of kinship that your tribe can achieve. Think deeply on this, Tribe Leader!

Communication styles are a more specific and targeted expression of the Platinum Rule. In addition to treating people the way they need to be treated, you also must communicate to them in the manner that works for them.

'Communication is the bridge between chaos and clarity.'

There are three *forms* of communication, verbal, non-verbal and visual. Understanding these three forms will help you give intentional, full spectrum communication.

There are also four different communication *styles* and mastering these will make your communication targeted and impactful.

The Three Forms of Communication
1. Verbal Communication
"Grasp the subject, the words will follow."
–Cato The Elder

Verbal communication is the most obvious form of communication but it is actually the least impactful especially regarding influence and retention of information. Verbal communication is still a central tool in your communication toolbox and ensuring that your words are clear, concise, correct, coherent and courteous will ensure maximum results. All these verbal communication factors can and should be improved because your ability to communicate effectively will dictate the success of your kinship system and all of its projects. It may be painful at first but listen to yourself talk on a zoom recording or other platform and you will immediately hear opportunities for improvement. You deserve this. Your people and projects demand it.

2. Nonverbal Communication

"The most important thing in communication is to hear what isn't being said."
-Peter Drucker

There are numerous studies devoted to the complex subject of nonverbal communication and they all agree that between 70% and 93% of all communication is nonverbal. This is very important for you, Tribe Leader!

How are you presenting your communication? How is your posture? Do you use hand gestures? Even your appearance carries more weight than your words and people who look stressed, unprepared and disheveled project a lack of confidence, expertise and authority. People who are fit, stand upright and maintain strong eye contact communicate a vast amount of information without a word being said. This is referred to as *command bearing* in the military. Your nonverbal language speaks volumes.

3. Visual communication

"Within your visual communication there will inevitably be information and meaning beyond the image itself. This makes visual communication a very powerful tool."
-Aldous Huxley

Visual forms of communication include maps, signs and other graphics that represent ideas and topics that are often too large or complex to be fully expressed in words alone. Humans are visual creatures and these visuals augment your communication. Use them.

The Four Communication Styles

In addition to the three *forms* of communication there are four main communication *styles:* analytical, intuitive, functional and personal. Like other versions of the platinum rule, every person has a preferred method of communication and delivering your message in that style will substantially improve the quality and impact of your message. Regardless of what your personal communication style is, if you are versatile enough to deliver your message in the style that works for your listener you will get greater results. Like everything else in leadership this will take practice but it will transform the success of your people and projects.

Active listening and watching the verbal and non-verbal communication forms of your people will give you all the information you need to determine their communication style. In addition to giving you clues about their active communication style, active listening itself is a key communication best practice.

Poor communicators are rarely actively listening and just waiting to reply. Don't be those people

Analytical Style
Analytical communicators are going to appreciate and use numbers, historical precedents and data. They will site sources and expect you to do the same. Measurable information and stats will carry vastly more weight with these members of your tribe than emotional statements.

The benefit of being able to access this analytical communication style is the ability to deal with emotional situations logically. Even when dealing with sensitive issues, analytical people will respond positively if there are stats and research to back up your topic. When dealing with analytical communicators come prepared or you will experience the downside of that communication style which can be dismissive and passive-aggressive. Don't take this personally, Tribe Leader, recommit to your thoughtful position or come back better prepared.

Intuitive Communication Style

Intuitive communicators are very expressive and want to discuss the big picture and vision of a topic. Unlike the analytical communicators, intuitives will reject getting bogged down in stats and granular details of a project. If you join them in the big picture level of the conversation you will discover that insights, innovation and creativity will begin to flow. Ideas and solutions happen quickly when working with an intuitive.

The challenge of conversation with intuitive communicators is avoiding mistakes that are often made by bypassing details and specifics. In addition, they can quickly become impatient and even overly assertive with a pace they feel is too slow. Keep them on track and don't let them take things personally.

Functional Communication Style

The functional communicator is all about results. They do not need the slow and detailed approach of the analytic or the visionary approach of the intuitive. The functional communicator wants to get to the next right step and the implementation of that step.

You will often find that communication itself is a frustrating use of time to the functional communicator who would rather be doing the topic at hand instead of discussing it. Be brief and be action oriented or you will discover the functional communicator will become impatient and even aggressive.

Personal Communication Style

Personal communicators often use emotions and feelings in their communication and see the act of communication as a part of a relationship. They want to know how you are *feeling* about the topic and the conversation itself. Personal communication will develop your interpersonal connections and kinship with your tribe because it focuses on the human aspect of the topic or project at hand. This can be a vital style to help you navigate personal challenges but it can also trap you in feelings instead of solutions and action. In addition, personal communicators can be threatened by other communication styles and become passive and acquiesce.

Communication is a relationship and in every relationship you can only control your part. Claim that part with great intentionality! Listen and watch actively so you can determine the communication style of your partner and do what you can to make that relationship communication work. This is a vital part of the Platinum Rule that powers kinship and sets the stage for the big challenges and results in the next phase of the Tribe Triangle.

Tribe leaders must write and speak

Choose one member of your inner circle and reflect on how they communicate. Are they analytic, intuitive, functional or personal communicators?

_____
_____
_____

What is one way you can improve the way you communicate with them?

_____
_____
_____

What is your communication style?

_____
_____
_____

STEP 25 UP THE TRIBE TRIANGLE:

The Large-Scale Power of Morale

"Morale is the capacity of a group of people to pull together persistently and consistently in pursuit of a common purpose."
Alexander H. Leighton

Morale is the confidence, enthusiasm and discipline of a person or group. It is the esprit de corps that is the capacity of a group to claim and maintain belief in a shared challenge (and the group itself) in the face of opposition and adversity.

Morale is applied optimism

Morale is often associated with sports teams and the military. These are both rare examples of existing honor-based cultures that used to typify the culture of tribe. In both sports and the military, cohesion and commitment to the shared vision, values and mission are central. Higher morale has been proven to be a competitive advantage that increases resiliency and commitment to a challenge.

Morale has been used in the military as a 'mission critical' measure of psychological readiness of troops. It also is a direct and powerful driver of performance of all organizations including families and business.

Morale has long been proven to have a direct effect on workplace productivity by driving increased engagement, overall productivity, and customer satisfaction. The Gallup Organization estimates that there are over 22 million American workers who are actively disengaged due to low morale which costs the economy over 350 billion dollars a year in lost productivity, high turnover and absenteeism.

It has long been recognized that morale helps stop surrender. This is as true in our families and business as it is in any other struggle in history. Fear and doubt kill more projects than defeat ever has.

Morale is a product of kinship. It is a downstream effect of all the aspects of the honor-based culture of the Tribe Triangle including the shared tribe vision, values and mission of the alignment phase as well as the trust, resiliency, kindness and friendship and the platinum rule of the kinship phase. The kinship behavior of authentic appreciation is a major factor in building and maintaining morale.

You cannot decree morale because it is a product of community cohesion. Like everything else on your journey up the Tribe Triangle it must be made and maintained by intentional and consistent leadership of you, the Head of Culture. In addition to be a powerful driver of overall success, your team's morale is also a powerful diagnostic tool to gauge the health of your culture. Low morale is a warning light on the dashboard of your tribe and it behooves you to look under the hood and at your leadership.

The number one cause of lack of morale in 2012 study by the US military is "ineffective leaders at senior levels". This is YOU, Tribe Leader. It is our duty to own the failures of our tribe but share the successes.

Morale is not endless and is connected to resiliency. Recovery from periods of stress is vital for morale to be sustained. If you fail to maintain your foundation of morale it will crumble for your tribe like a sandcastle. Morale begins with you.

Tribe leaders must write and speak

What is a challenging family or work project in which your people are disengaged from and avoiding?

_____

_____

_____

What morale drivers from the alignment level of the Tribe Triangle can you shore up? (Shared vision for the future, shared core values or shared collaboration of mission?)

_____

_____

_____

What morale drivers from the kinship level of the Tribe Triangle are at your disposal? (Resiliency, altruism, friendship, communication or appreciation?)

_____

_____

_____

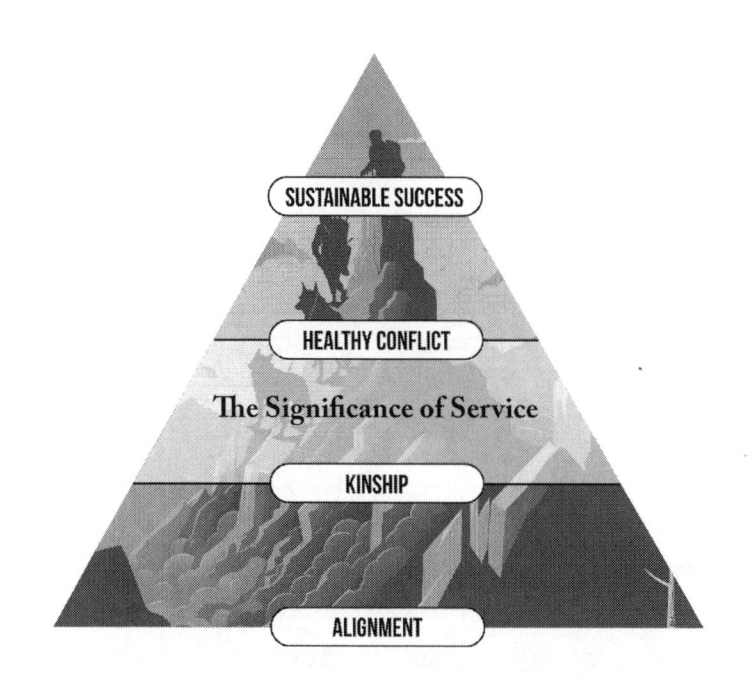

STEP 26 UP THE TRIBE TRIANGLE:

The Significance of Service

"Service to others is the rent you pay for your room here on earth."

–Muhammad Ali

Service echoes through every level of the Tribe Triangle and is a core aspect of humanity itself. It is the capstone of the Kinship function of your tribe. Service is a key component of an honor-based culture because it inherently involves a duty to people and projects that are larger than ourselves. All forms of heroism in human history are performed in the service of others.

Service is a form of applied altruism and contributes to all other aspects of the kinship level of the Tribe Triangle including morale, kindness, friendships and appreciation. *Kinship culminates in service.*

In addition to being the apex behavior of the kinship level of our journey, it also establishes the behavior of the next level of the Tribe Triangle which is Healthy Conflict. We cannot successfully engage with all the greatness of healthy conflict without exploring and implementing service first.

In our individual-centric, pride-based culture, service is viewed as an optional, discretionary act that we *may* get to when we have the free time or resources. It is much more than that. Service is a survival protocol that enables us to persevere and succeed in the face of adversity.

As we discussed earlier in step 18, when the famous anthropologist Margaret Mead was asked what the earliest example of civilization was, her response was not pottery, stone tools or fire, it was a healed femur. Breaking your leg in the wilderness for almost every species on earth is a death sentence except for humans (and wolves which are our ancient ally). We regularly see healed bones in ancient human and wolf skeletons and this is evidence of the altruism of service. The tribe had to make tremendous sacrifices of movement, safety and resources to take care of an injured member.

> *"Helping someone else through difficulty is where civilization starts."*
> *-Margaret Mead*

Humans are only powerful, resilient and successful when they are in aligned groups in kinship systems. Remember Ubuntu; *I am because we are, and we are because I am.* We are here to serve others and be served by others. We can see and feel the dysfunction of our pride-based culture in the obsession with individual rights being prioritized over the need of collective responsibility or service.

The movement towards almost complete self-interest and the culture of "Me" is visible in almost every facet of everyday life. It shows up as short-term materialism and immediate gratification competitiveness. Unfortunately, this attempt to get our individual needs met is doing completely the opposite and people have never felt more alone, isolated and lonely than ever before. This lack of belonging and service is the upstream rot leading to the skyrocketing mental and emotional symptoms of clinical anxiety, depression, addiction and suicide. People need other people and to do that they need to serve other people.

"The best way to find yourself is to lose yourself in the service of others."
– Mahatma Gandhi

Leaders are especially impacted by the lack of service in a company and culture because leaders must embrace a purpose and a vision beyond themselves to find meaning in the sacrifices that are inherent in leadership. The service to others, and things larger than ourselves, is a universal component in every faith in history. **Service is faith in action.**

Service must also include service to *self*, Tribe Leader. If we continue to pour out, we will eventually have nothing left to give in the service of others. Sometimes this means simply getting appreciated which is something leaders do not get enough of. This dynamic may be part of your culture norms or perhaps it is because it appears that you do not need it. Both of these factors are worth investigating and you may find that as Head of Culture, you are the source of both. Recommit to the public and transparent modeling of service to yourself, your tribe and the world.

Tribe leaders must write and speak

What service does your family or company provide the community or world?

_____

_____

_____

Is this clearly reflected in your shared vision statement?

_____

_____

_____

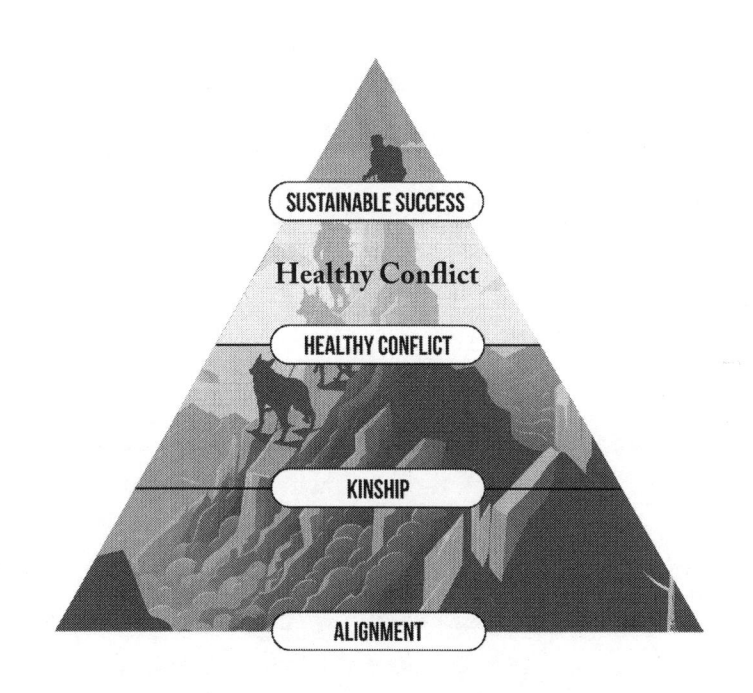

PHASE 3 UP THE TRIBE TRIANGLE:

Introduction to the Healthy Conflict

Before I start on a culture or leadership development engagement with a company I do an organizational needs assessment. This involves exploring the challenges that they know they are facing as well as the desired state they are working to achieve. This list regularly includes increased innovation, accountability and risk-taking with their team. My first question in response to their wish list is: *"are you prepared to deal with failure and conflict?"*

Innovation includes and actually *requires* failure. These initial failures are built into the innovation process and if leadership does not identify this and prepare to deal with it in short or medium term they will never embrace the power and payoff of innovation in the long term. The same is true for establishing a culture where people hold themselves and each other accountable for their goals and behavior as well as speaking their truth, risk-taking and almost every other form of success.

All of these challenges involve conflict. There will be conflict with ourselves as we face setbacks and there will be conflict between your people as they engage with each other, their work, goals and their standards.

In all traditional and established honor-based cultures conflict is normalized and accepted as an unavoidable price of success. Players compete in the weight room and practice field so they can win on the field. The same is true for the military and every other example of a high performing industry or team.

Organizations that attempt to implement the profit and success drivers that exist in the Healthy Conflict phase of the Tribe Triangle without establishing the rock-solid foundation of Alignment and the trust, safety and resiliency of Kinship are sailing into the storm without a solid ship and a trained crew. Take good notes and do your homework on this phase of your culture creation, brave Tribe Leader!

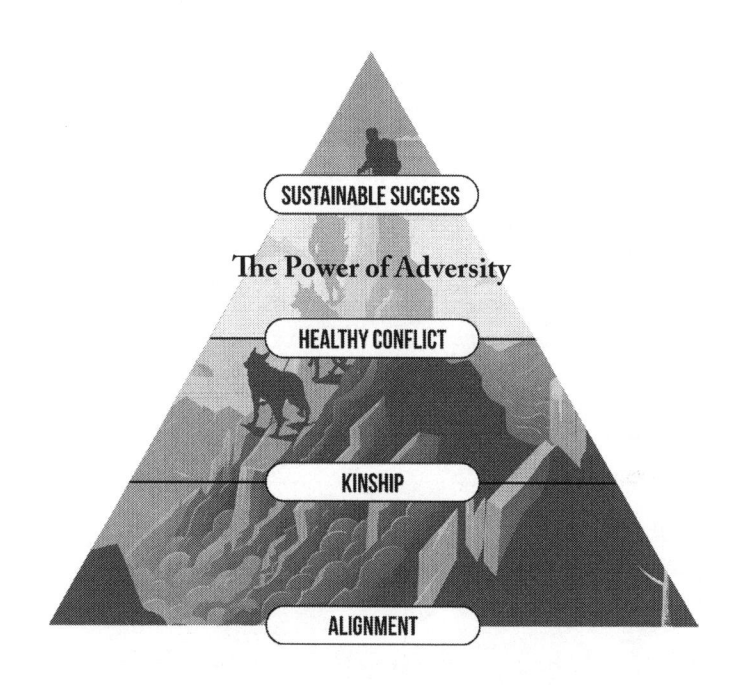

STEP 27 UP THE TRIBE TRIANGLE:

The Power of Adversity

"No man is more unhappy than he who never faces adversity, for he is not permitted to prove himself."
—Seneca

Humans are designed for extreme adversity and challenge. Every single one of us is the product of ancestors who persevered through ice ages, apocalyptic floods, droughts and famine. Through most of our history on earth, not being eaten was a major daily challenge. All this resiliency is literally built into our genes and we are the children of relentless survivors who refused to quit because quitting meant death along with your whole family and tribe.

The primary source of resiliency in the face of hardship was the collective power of the tribe and every factor of the kinship level of the Tribe Triangle is a source of resiliency. Kinship is an indispensable survival skill because it makes us feel safe.

Being safe and *feeling* safe are very different things and making your people feel safe is your challenge because healthy conflict is a product of the *feeling* of safety.

"I am because we are, and we are because I am" should be the mantra of every person who is preparing to face challenges successfully.

We are currently living in a magical age of climate-controlled environments and vehicles that allow us to avoid the discomfort of walking and escalators that allow us to avoid the discomfort of climbing. We are blind to the miracle of endless clean water that comes out of pipes in the wall and the strange challenge of having so much food that obesity is a larger health challenge than starvation.

Instead of ushering in a golden age of humanity this lack of adversity is causing a collapse into anxiety, depression, addiction and suicide. We have not been liberated from the genuine stresses of survival but are instead dying of stress and lifestyle-related illnesses of heart disease, cancer, strokes and diabetes.

Discomfort is now viewed as 'bad' and evidence that something has gone wrong instead of a normal condition of life. Again, we are living in deeply artificial times and artificial times require artificial means. We must learn to embrace the healthy conflict of adversity to reclaim our resiliency, organizational success and both physical and psychological well-being.

Normalizing healthy conflict and adversity is a steep challenge for your family and organization and must be led and modeled by you, Tribe Leader. Here are several categories and best practices to reclaim the sustainable success of thriving in adversity.

Healthy conflict encompasses a wide range of success drivers including risk-taking, innovation, accountability and conflict resolution. Creating a healthy relationship with healthy conflict is the process of developing resiliency. *The ability to engage with healthy conflict is the ability to compete successfully now and evolve successfully for the future.*

Like every level of the Tribe Triangle, Healthy Conflict cannot be decreed. It must be made and maintained by vigilant and regular recommitment of all the culture components below it. If you or your team find yourselves struggling with any of the factors related to the risk-taking, innovation and accountability of healthy conflict, do a quick inventory of the foundational components of your honor-based culture.

Components of Honor Alignment
- Shared vision
- Shared values
- Shared mission
- Mission Transparency
- Reciprocity
- Brand clarification
- Change management

Components of Kinship
- Resiliency
- Sustainability
- Kindness
- Altruism
- Platinum Rule
- Friendships
- Trust and Safety
- Appreciation
- Communication

The reason that issues related to healthy conflict cannot be decreed and only established with the hard work above, is the simple fact that they are *hard*. Significant growth and advancement of all sorts is always hard. Not because of the resource output that it requires (but that is also true), but hard because it will always involve the death of the old way of doing things and that is psychologically deeply uncomfortable. *The establishment of new behaviors and practices requires the death of old accepted habits.*

Habits are comfortable and efficient, that is all. They are not designed for growth and new practices and procedures are very energy and resource demanding. Running is hard, walking is easy. Sitting down is easier still. Quitting is always close and always available.

All life including the life of your family and organization will always tend towards comfort and ultimately, entropy. Your job as Tribe Leader is to shovel coal into the furnace of success and to continue fighting for growth. This entire section of the Tribe Triangle is what you need to do to win in this arena.

Growth and advancement are also hard because they involve conflict with accepted procedures, roles and identities. This process will always trigger and threaten many people because it is the death of their old story and regardless of how beautiful and powerful the vision of the new phoenix is, no one looks forward to burning to death.

Hold your vision! This journey of growth will require you to climb the mountain of conflict. **No one accidentally walks uphill and no mountain is climbed accidentally.**
Healthy conflict can only be honestly discussed, explored and implemented after establishment of the alignment foundation and the trust and safety of kinship.

Tribe leaders must write and speak

Where is your family or organization struggling with growth or change?

_____

_____

_____

What components of Alignment or Kinship are lacking in your culture? Write them down for yourself and speak them to your leaders and partners. This is the beginning of Healthy Conflict which is an unavoidable step towards thriving.

Components of Honor Alignment
- Shared vision
- Shared values
- Shared mission
- Mission Transparency
- Reciprocity
- Brand clarification
- Change management

Components of Kinship
- Resiliency
- Sustainability
- Kindness
- Altruism
- Platinum Rule
- Friendships
- Trust and Safety
- Appreciation
- Communication

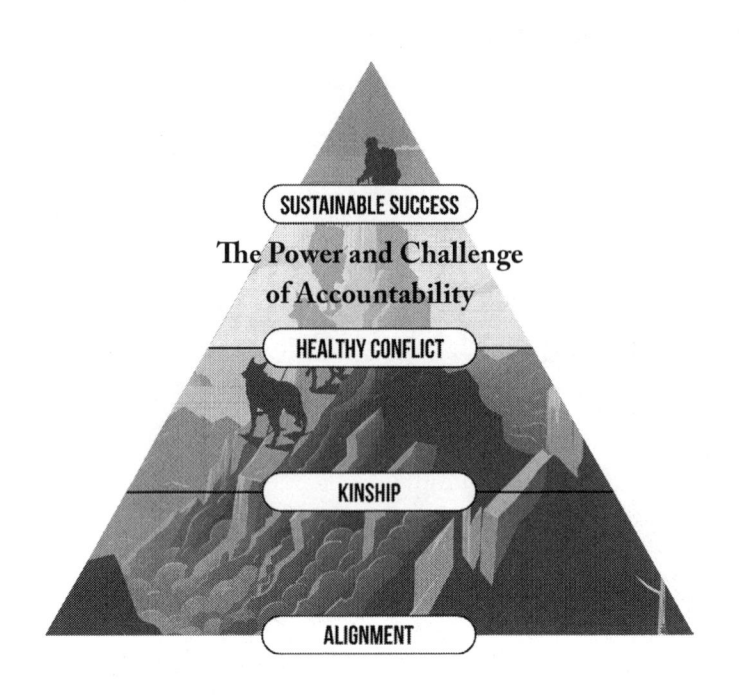

STEP 28 UP THE TRIBE TRIANGLE:

The Power and Challenge of Accountability

"We are not afraid of failure as much as we are afraid of what success will require from us."

–Philip Folsom

Everything great will be hard. This axiom holds true for all your personal development journeys as well as the collective path of leading your tribe towards greatness. At some point there will be resistance from both you and your team.

If there is one magic tool in your leadership arsenal to sustainably overcome this inevitable resistance, it is *accountability*. Like everything else in this level of the Tribe Triangle, using that tool is very simple but very hard and you *will* get better at it with practice!

Willpower and brave intentions will not be enough to sustain you through adversity. Sooner or later, you will become tired, distracted and overwhelmed and you will revert back to whatever baseline of behavior where you and your team normally operate at. Leveling up your operating system from that baseline of habit to the new level of practice is the process of going from efficiency to growth and it will require a tremendous increase in energy. This heavy lift must be shared and that collective burden is called accountability.

Accountability is collective responsibility to a shared goal. It is the engine that connects intention and commitment to actual results

Everything in the Healthy Conflict level of the Tribe Triangle is an immediate precursor to competitive greatness and excellence and none of it is free. In addition, every step in this stage of your culture development journey will be impossible to decree or mandate; it must be made and maintained by your previous work in the *alignment* and *kinship* phases.

Accountability is a byproduct of all the components of alignment and kinship. This is especially true in the following three categories which are all indispensable for implementing accountability in your tribe:
1. Commitment to a clear shared purpose or 'why'.
2. Modeling clear transparency with goals and expectations.
3. Establishing clear communication and avoiding assumptions.

Without these early-stage culture norms, you will not be able to make or maintain successful and ongoing accountability. This is especially true in this era of increasing remote work where people are experiencing more disengagement and disconnection from their organization's shared culture.

The difference between accountability and shame or blame

If you attempt to implement accountability in your team without first establishing the shared alignment and kinship functions of the Tribe Triangle, it will often look and feel like shame or blame. Both shame/blame and accountability deal with external feedback and increased pressure on process and results. This process is both powerful and dangerous.

If we have a shared mission and the safety of kinship, that feedback and pressure feels like support

Without shared alignment and kinship, that increased pressure and feedback feels like shame and blame

Implementing accountability without the crippling experience of shame or blame is the reason why accountability is only successful in the Healthy Conflict level of your journey up the Tribe Triangle. There are several other vital factors to consider when implementing accountability.

Accountability involves *responsibility* and *consequences*. Consequences are powerful and should be a healthy component to any project. The natural world is filled with consequences which are usually immediate and non-negotiable. Now, we are often shielded from the consequences of our decisions by the artificial culture of comfort that we are born into. Establishing intentional consequences is a part of rejoining the natural order of the world. Again, we must be mindful of how our people are responding to these consequences and make sure they are driving engagement not eroding it.

One of the greatest fears of establishing and implementing accountability as a leader is that we won't be liked. Leaders are often not liked in the short term but it is vastly better to be respected and successful than liked. Heavy lies the crown and this is another reason that successful accountability only happens in the Healthy Conflict level of the Tribe Triangle.

Accountability should be skillfully aimed at the following three primary categories. Consider how you are leveraging your leadership to drive engagement, hit deadlines and celebrate success. These three categories are what everyone on the team should answer to and, like everything else, this is modeled by you first.

"Accountability is the measure of a leader's height."
-Jeffery Benjamin

Accountability to Purpose - This is the shared vision of your tribe. Accountability should always include this larger sense of duty to something that is aspirational and significant. When we set and honor goals, we must make sure they are connected back to the larger shared 'why' of the organization. In many ways, striving toward meaningful things carries its own accountability of honor, obligation and duty because it provides inherent meaning.

Accountability to Performance - Successful accountability must be focused on both *results* as well as *progress* and they are two very different things. *Results* are mission outcomes that ensures that the entire organization is moving forward toward our shared vision. *Progress*, on the other hand, is focused on effort that is based on shared values. Too much focus on results can lead to unethical behavior and cutting corners to achieve an outcome. Make sure that you are acknowledging and rewarding the struggle of moving forward in the face of adversity not just the results. Resiliency and character are also examples of performance.

Accountability to People - The most important form of accountability is the responsibility we have to each other. People are your most important resource and the behavior we model and enforce is central to our sustainable success. Accountability must acknowledge and drive behaviors that are in alignment to the shared values of your family or organization. People-based accountability should also involve honoring and enforcing transparency behavior, collaboration and the mode and cadence of communication on projects.

Tribe leaders must write and speak

Where are you seeing performance or people-based challenges in your family or organization? These will be visible by a lack of progress and results as well as a lack of engagement and morale.

_____

_____

_____

What form of clarity and accountability can you implement to move those needles?

_____

_____

_____

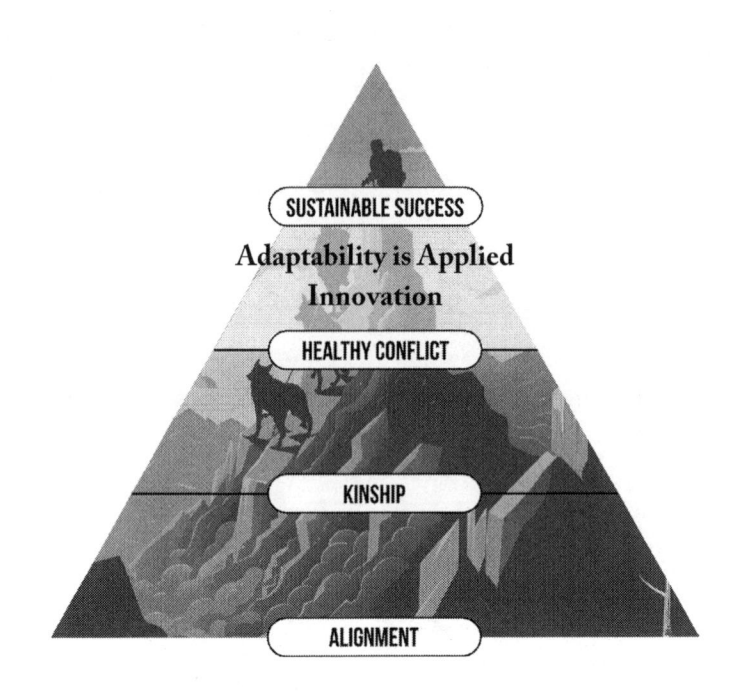

STEP 29 UP THE TRIBE TRIANGLE:

Adaptability is Applied Innovation

"Evolution is not survival of the fittest it is survival of the most adaptable."
–Philip Folsom

We explored the importance and best practices of change management in step 13 but innovation is another animal entirely. Innovation is intentional risk taking and revolution of ideas, projects and practices. Innovation is more than creativity which is just thinking of new ideas. Innovation is actually doing them. **Innovation is intentional and accelerated adaptation.**

Corporate clients often come to me with a wish list of culture development outcomes. Almost all of them come straight out of the Healthy Conflict level of the Tribe Triangle and innovation is at the top of that list. When asked to help companies create a culture of innovation, I always respond by asking: "are you willing, prepared and strong enough to lose and fail?" Risk and failure are the unavoidable costs of innovation. Innovation is the ability to see past the threat of change and see the opportunity.

> *"There is no innovation without failure. Period."*
> *-Brene Brown*

Failure is the lifeblood of innovation, and this is why it cannot be successfully activated until the Healthy Conflict phase of culture creation. We cannot innovate if we cannot incorporate failure in the process *and* the result. We must learn to hunt and embrace honest failure, breakdowns and limits in the pursuit of growth. Successful innovation is a product of experience. It is applied creativity. The enemy of innovation is judgement, control, comfort and safety. All of these things must be sacrificed on the altar of innovation for it to flourish in you family and team.

Innovative companies must be prepared for the inevitable conflict of losing and adversity because most innovation fails. You, as Head of Culture must model and support and learn from these failures. This means popping the hood and taking a look at all the culture drivers that create Healthy Conflict. If you are committed to innovation, you must build this philosophy into both your alignment and kinship components.

If innovation is a priority for you and your team, you must include those components in your core values. These growth-driving behaviors will power risk-taking, collaboration and all the other foundations of sustainable innovation.

Here is an example of a corporate values statement that champions a culture of innovation:

> *"We have an incredibly high tolerance for non-repetitive mistakes made in the pursuit of excellence."*

In addition to being intentional with your vision, mission and values from the alignment phase, almost the entire stable of kinship functions will also power innovation. Focus on celebrating differences, boosting morale and trust and safety because they are all indispensable for shaping an environment of innovation.

> *"The only constant is change."*
> *Heraclitus*

Innovation is playing offense instead of defense. A football team that is built around offense is going to get scored on a lot and there will be many incomplete passes, especially in the beginning. That's the nature of throwing the ball downfield. Most passes are incomplete but the ones that do connect gain lots of yards and score lots of points. Are you ready and resilient enough to withstand that assault on your confidence and numbers?

Many of my clients are looking for the quick fix, magic bullet of success and this includes innovation. Innovation looks quick but is actually the product of long-term, intentional investment in your culture.

We must normalize risk-taking and growth as well as the safety and resiliency required to persevere through failure. Fail fast. Fail forward.

Tribe leaders must write and speak

When was the last time you fully committed to something and failed? This question is probably harder than it seems because you may have not *fully committed* to a risk recently. None of us do because that involves failure.

_____

_____

_____

Were you transparent in that failure? This is how we model and normalize innovation to our families and teams.

_____

_____

_____

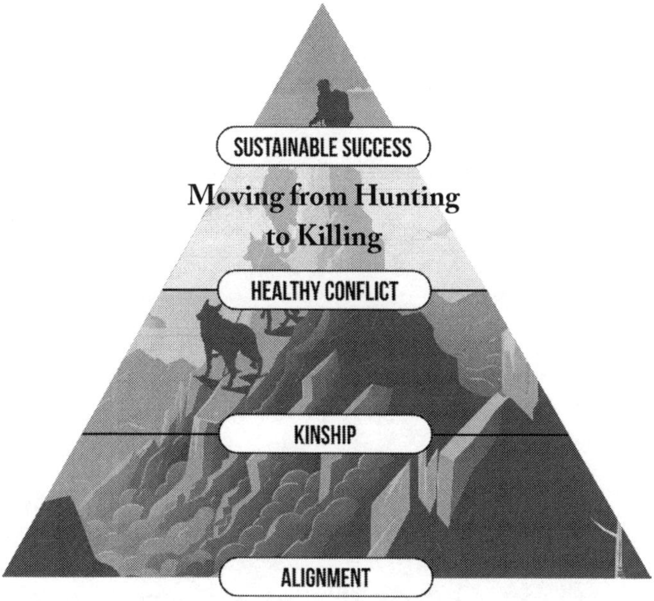
SUSTAINABLE SUCCESS
Moving from Hunting to Killing
HEALTHY CONFLICT
KINSHIP
ALIGNMENT

STEP 30 UP THE TRIBE TRIANGLE:

Moving from Hunting to Killing

"You can starve to death reading cookbooks."

A signature of the Healthy Conflict phase is the ability to move from intention to action. It is decisively entering the challenging arena of measurable success. There are great risks here but also great rewards and making that journey requires an understanding of the things that will stop you and your team as well as how you will benefit.

"The cave you fear to enter contains the treasure you seek."
-Joseph Campbell

The transition from intention to action will show up in every aspect of your culture including your people, your processes and your projects. An example of this evolution is in step 29 where we explored Innovation which is *applied* creativity. This is a vital distinction because people and teams do not become successful by creatively playing with new ideas. People and teams become successful by *implementing* new ideas. This involves commitment and often, failure.

The progression from the perceived safety of uncommitted creativity to the perceived risk of innovation can only be made successfully at the Healthy Conflict stage in your culture creation. We need the foundation of shared alignment and the support of kinship to make innovation sustainable.

Both hunting and reading cookbooks are examples of creativity and exploring your options. This is an indispensable component to your tribe's toolbox. The mindset of creativity involves hunting as many available options as possible and cross referencing them with what is best and what is doable with the ingredients you have.

When hunting or reading cookbooks we want to open the aperture of our eyes and mind to bring in as many choices as possible. This is the process of *concentration* which is additive. It means *gathering things together*. This is another form of creativity.

The opposite of concentration is *focus*. Instead of being additive, like concentration, focus is subtractive. It means removing everything besides the one focal point or singular priority.

- *Concentrating* is gathering information, options, creativity and hunting.
- *Focusing* is deciding, committing and killing.

Creativity is a privileged position to be in because it involves freedom and preferences. Hunting and reading cookbooks is optional. Killing and eating is mandatory. At some point you must actually open the pantry, start pulling ingredients out and turn on the stove.

Killing and competing is the acknowledgement that at some point, we must commit to a course of action to get a required result. When the game is on the line and the contract is at stake, we all must pick a target and put our chips on the table.

Waiting is not free and neither is commitment. The cost for commitment is possible short-term failure. The cost of waiting is guaranteed long-term failure. Pick your price, Tribe Leader.

There are many costs for procrastination. The first is loss of competitiveness. Whether you acknowledge it or not, you are already in the arena and competing. This is happening financially, professionally, socially and in every other area of your life. People who are waiting for *when they're ready* or *when they have the time* are not standing still, they are falling behind.

> "A man who procrastinates in his choice will inevitably have his choice made for him by circumstance."
> –Hunter S. Thompson

Fish or cut bait, Tribe Leader. This means either get about deciding and committing to an action or do something useful in support of that action. Hunt as long as you can but kill when you must. Do not wait. Writing ideas, goals and intentions down and speaking them to other people are indispensable transitions from hunting to killing.

Tribe leaders must write and speak

What is a hard but important action or decision that you have been putting off?

_____
_____
_____

What is the cost of that procrastination?

_____
_____
_____

What is the benefit of committed action?

_____
_____
_____

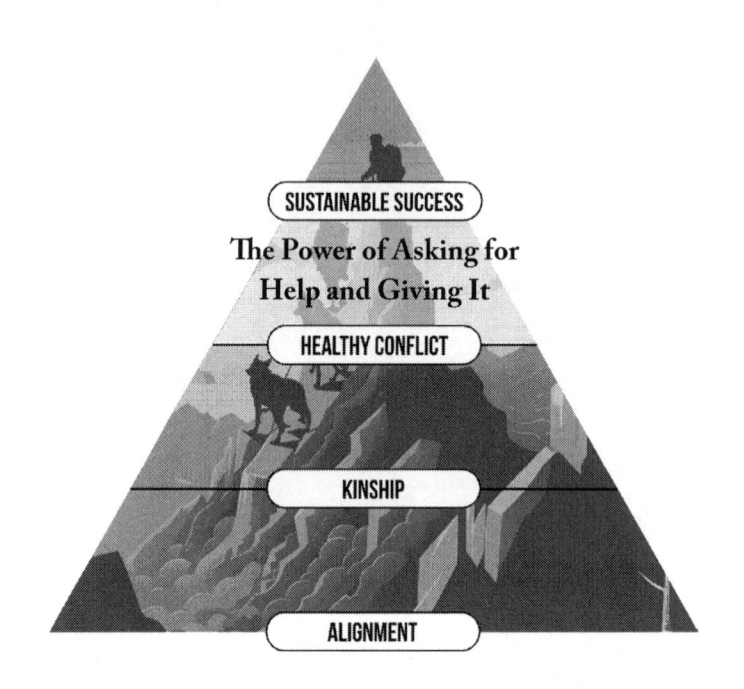

STEP 31 UP THE TRIBE TRIANGLE:

The Power of Asking for Help and Giving It

"Our prime purpose in this life is to help others."
–Dali Lama

Asking for help and giving it is the most powerful expression of collaboration. Like everything else in the Healthy Conflict phase of the Tribe Triangle, it is very simple and also very hard.

Authentically asking for help is truly fearful for most people, and, in a pride-based culture of individuals, this is often too risky to engage in. Asking for help in a society of lone wolves is a psychological and professional minefield. It opens the vulnerability door to judgement, shame, inadequacy and a whole host of factors behind the universal imposter syndrome experienced by almost every person today.

Trying to implement a culture of asking for help is a common and well-intentioned strategy for people who have never actually been in charge of people. Those of us who have managed many people and projects over the years realize that people say they would ask for help if they need it but rarely actually do in our culture.
Students almost never actually use professor's office hours.
Employees rarely use a manager's 'open door' policies.

There are three primary strategies for making and maintaining a culture that can ask for help and give it. They are all valuable and well worth the return on investment because of the increased morale and sustainable performance that comes from this heightened level of collaboration.

The first strategy for creating an environment of mutual aid is to include it in your shared values. This is a no brainer but be aware that every value contains the cost of other values that are not in the top three. For example, when we establish and model asking for help and giving it we risk eroding the values of independence, autonomy and self-determination. This can be mitigated by the inclusion of more mission-oriented values as well as reinforcing your shared vision which is inherently task oriented. Be very intentional in the choices of your tribe values for they dictate your destiny.

The second strategy also comes from reflecting back on your culture alignment foundation and doubling down on your mission transparency.

When you model sharing the personal and shared challenges of your mission, you are laying the groundwork for asking for help because it engages collaboration. *Collaboration is the bedrock of asking for help and giving it.*

Increased collaboration also activates reciprocity which is the engine of kinship and all aspects of the Kinship level of the Tribe Triangle contribute to the trust and safety required for your people to ask for help and give it.

The third strategy of getting people to ask for help is to get them to *give help first* before asking for it.

Even in honor-based cultures asking for help is challenging and the military has a battle-tested strategy to overcome this. When I was in the army, we were taught that our duty was to look after the other 10 men in our platoon before ourselves. This seems counter-intuitive but it meant that there were 10 other soldiers looking after each one of us. This strategy acknowledged the fact that people will not generally ask for help and if the cultural norm was to give help it automatically addressed this. I have personally seen this work in many organizations over my career.

Create a culture where people reach in because they may never reach out

We can see all these strategies in action in the ancient ritual of the communal barn raising. This is an example of a significant and meaningful project that no one person could ever accomplish alone. If you and your family or work team are truly pursuing your shared, aspirational vision, you will be facing this scale of challenge. Take note, Tribe Leader, we cannot hunt big game alone.

Barn raising was a common practice in rural America throughout the last two hundred years when the barn was a central but costly pillar of the farming community. Raising a barn required more labor than any one family could muster and it became an established norm (shared value) that the entire honor-based community would gather to conduct the heavy lift of establishing the structure.

This process included the entire Shared Mission sequence of the Alignment phase of the Tribe Triangle. *Transparency* was required by sharing the need and logistics of the event. *Collaboration* of the community was the result, and *reciprocity* was activated by returning the favor when it was time for your neighbor's barn to be raised. All these success drivers of alignment powered kinship and sustainable success for the entire community. What barns in your family or organization need raising?

There is one more vital aspect of asking for help and giving it; it feels good to give help to people. It makes the giver feel valuable, powerful and important.

On Christmas, almost everyone enjoys watching other people open presents that they are giving them more than opening presents themselves. There is ancient human altruism and honor in this small, modern moment. By letting your team help you, you are not only benefiting from their assistance but also modeling this central norm of high-performing teams. Celebrate the assists as much as the score.

> *"Refusing to ask for help when you need it*
> *is refusing someone the chance to be helpful."*
> *–Ric Ocasek*

Tribe leaders must write and speak

When was the last time you genuinely needed help in your family or work team? Did you ask for help?

_____

_____

_____

Has there been a time that your people have failed at a project because they didn't ask for help?

_____

_____

_____

What was the cause of this and how can you upgrade your culture to create more assistance sharing?

- Values
- Transparency on needs and communication
- Giving help first

_____

_____

_____

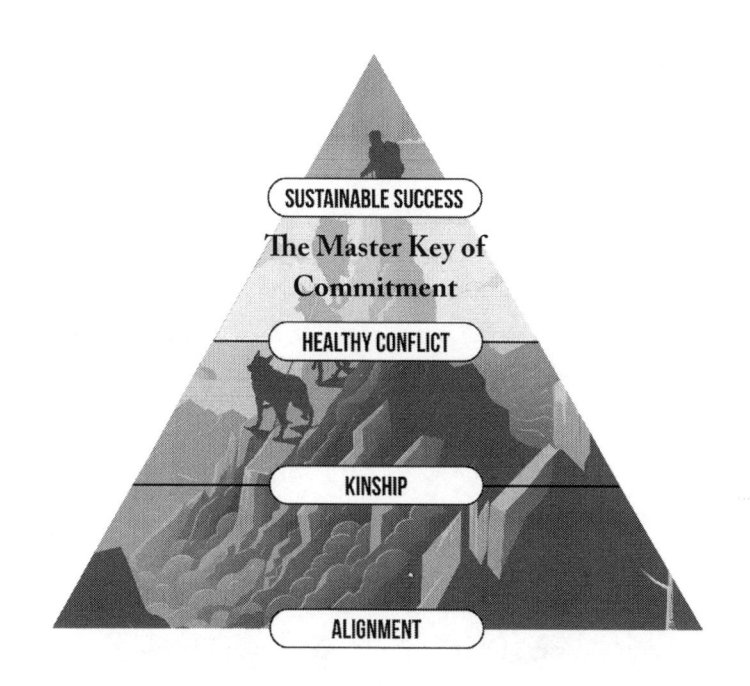

STEP 32 UP THE TRIBE TRIANGLE:

The Master Key of Commitment

"Burn the boats."
–*General Julius Caesar*

Commitment is *'the state or quality of being dedicated to a cause or activity'*. In both the family and workplace, commitment drives growth, engagement and motivation. Organizational commitment is one of the most important drivers of employee satisfaction and employee retention. These drive overall business performance and profitability. Commitment is vital for sustainable success in all areas of your life.

Like everything else at this level of the Tribe Triangle, commitment cannot be decreed and takes time and *intentional work* to develop. Commitment is a byproduct of all the culture investments you have made earlier in the Alignment and Kinship levels. **Commitment is created from culture before it drives culture.**

Once commitment begins to be expressed in your team, it starts driving the other culture components and is a proven factor in meeting goals and staying aligned to your shared vision. No great goal is ever met in the short term and commitment is vital for that journey to the Sustainable Success level of your family and organization.

> *"Most people fail, not because of lack of desire, but because of lack of commitment."*
> *-Vince Lombardi*

Employee retention is currently one of the greatest challenges of organizations. In almost all organizations, leaders are struggling to keep their team together and engaged. This low commitment challenge is exacerbated by the movement towards remote work and the quick-fix culture of instant gratification that leads employees to jump from company to company in search of the meaning that only exists in long term commitment. The internet is a powerful tool and resource but it is also a source of distraction and commitment erosion at work where an increasing number of employees surf the web and even search for other jobs instead of persevering at the shared mission at hand.

A committed team will become an autonomous and self-directed team. Commitment requires full buy-in of your shared vision and mission. When people are committed, they tend to own goals, find the intrinsic motivation to search for solutions and learn from setbacks and failures. This process is how all legitimate human development happens. Committed people either win or they learn and instead of looking at failure as final it becomes just another step on the path toward success. This is an example of applied resiliency.

Committed people fail forward

If we attempt to establish commitment before the resiliency that only happens from kinship culture, defeat can feel final. People take setbacks personally and they will find ways to avoid these challenges. You will know this is happening when you see and feel complacency in your team. They will be focused on numbers and dates instead of the process and journey that is linked to the significance of your shared vision. Your people must have safety and trust in you, each other, and the organization for commitment to become available to them. Commitment will appear in relationships as well as projects and this is an expression of kinship in action.

"Trust brings a higher level of communication and a higher level of commitment and accountability."
–Bruce Arians

You will know you have successfully achieved commitment when morale, creativity and innovation appear. There will be more engagement and that engagement will be intrinsically motivated instead of management motivated. People who are committed to a shared and inspiring goal and vision will automatically search for new ways to achieve that end. You can fast track commitment by including perseverance or other commitment drivers in the norms of your culture. These are your shared values that drive the thought process and decision-making hierarchy of your team.

"Stay committed to your decisions, but stay flexible to your approach."
-Tony Robbins

Without commitment, your team will struggle with engagement, resiliency and all other forms of sustainable success. Like everything else on this journey up the Tribe Triangle, commitment must be modeled by you, Tribe Leader. For you to lead your team on the noble but endless path toward your vision, you must stay engaged, resilient and committed and do this transparently. Your people may not always listen to you, but they are always watching.

"Commitment is what transforms a promise into a reality.'
-Abraham Lincoln

Tribe leaders must write and speak

Where are you seeing a lack of autonomy and motivation on your team or projects? These are symptoms of a lack of commitment.

_____
_____
_____

To increase the engagement and innovation that only comes from commitment you will need to find out which culture components are missing.

Are you transparently modeling commitment?

_____
_____
_____

Is your team bought in to your shared vision or does your team need a recommitment? This will be an ongoing process.

_____
_____
_____

Does your team have enough trust in you and each other that commitment and innovation-driven risks are normalized?

_____
_____
_____

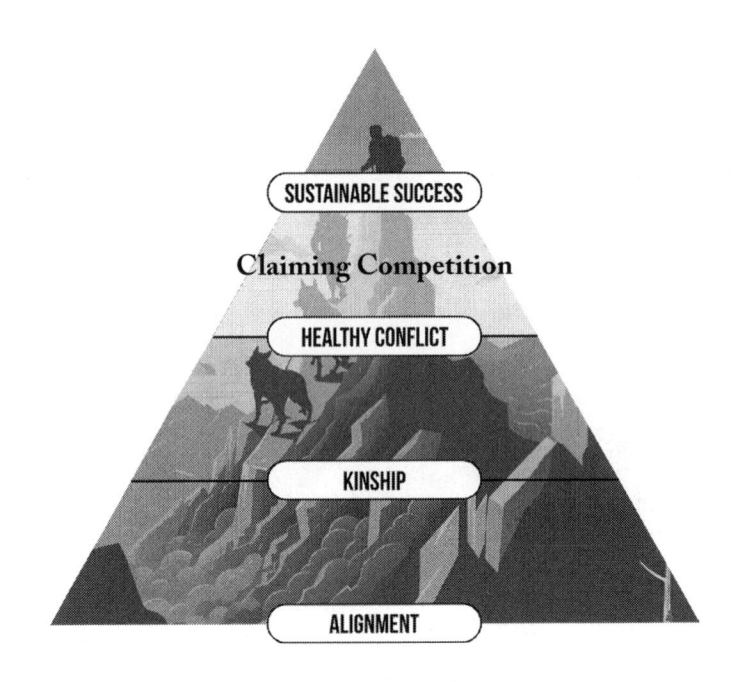

STEP 33 UP THE TRIBE TRIANGLE:

Claiming Competition

"Competition is the best form of motivation."

–Cordae

At some point in your personal and professional journey you will need to get in the arena and compete. This may be for a position, market share or sales. This journey into competition carries a tremendous energy for overall improvement but also contains the potential for damage if not handled intentionally and skillfully.

Competitive environments and industries demand that the customer's needs or concerns are met and this pressure drives innovation and improvements in quality of products and services. Competition is also a primary driver of many other components of sustainable success including improved systems that increase efficiency. The need to compete is the mother of all forms of invention and innovation. *Creativity is not competitive but innovation is.*

Along with the internal organizational upgrades that competition brings to your organization or family, there is also an undeniable benefit to society overall. When organizations compete it brings increased reliability, lower prices and drives innovation which benefits everyone. Others win when we progress and compete. This is capitalism.

"No competition, no progress."
-Bela Karolyi

In addition to improvements of products and procedures, competition also drives a deeper understanding about ourselves, our brand and our careers. To be successful in competition, we will be driven to research and deepen our knowledge of not only our services and products but our competition as well.

Competition forces an honest inventory and assessment of your own culture including every aspect of the Tribe Triangle. Struggle will force clarity of your shared vision, the efficacy of your shared values and the way you conduct your shared missions.

Competition will test and clarify every aspect of you as a leader and the culture you create. This exploration of who you are and what your culture is will be your ultimate competitive advantage as well as your legacy.

> *"Know thy enemy and know yourself; in a hundred battles, you will never be defeated. When you are ignorant of the enemy but know yourself, your chances of winning or losing are equal. If ignorant both of your enemy and of yourself, you are sure to be defeated in every battle."*
> *–Sun Tzu*

Competition is the great driver of improvement in all areas but it comes at a cost including increased stress which leads to a host of negative mental, emotional and physical challenges. The pressures of internal competition can also threaten the integrity of your entire culture. Not managing competition skillfully can lead to an erosion of transparency, communication and organizational values.

When competition trumps collaboration you should immediately stop, redirect and recommit to your pillars of culture

Collaboration is better than competition because it's a win-win for everyone in the arena and opens up the potential for alliances and sustainable success instead of short-term success. There will almost always be some sort of blow back when competing because when we are playing to win then someone must lose. Dealing with loss is always hard but not always necessary if you explore all avenues of collaboration first.

A good guiding principle for the distinction between collaboration and competition is to always cooperate internally and compete externally. Where is that incredibly important line between us and them? How much control do you have over where that line is drawn? You may discover that you have more control over collaboration, cooperation and alliances than you think.

"Don't fight a battle if you don't gain anything by winning."
−George S. Patton

Tribe leaders must write and speak

Collaboration makes us better, but competition makes us faster. What is a project in your family or organization that is moving too slowly?
___
___
___

Competition will accelerate this project. How can you implement healthy competition to facilitate this growth? Who is your competition?
___
___
___

In your existing competition, where does the opportunity to collaborate or form an alliance exist?
___
___
___

What is the cost and benefit from that cooperation? What is the next step towards it?
___
___
___

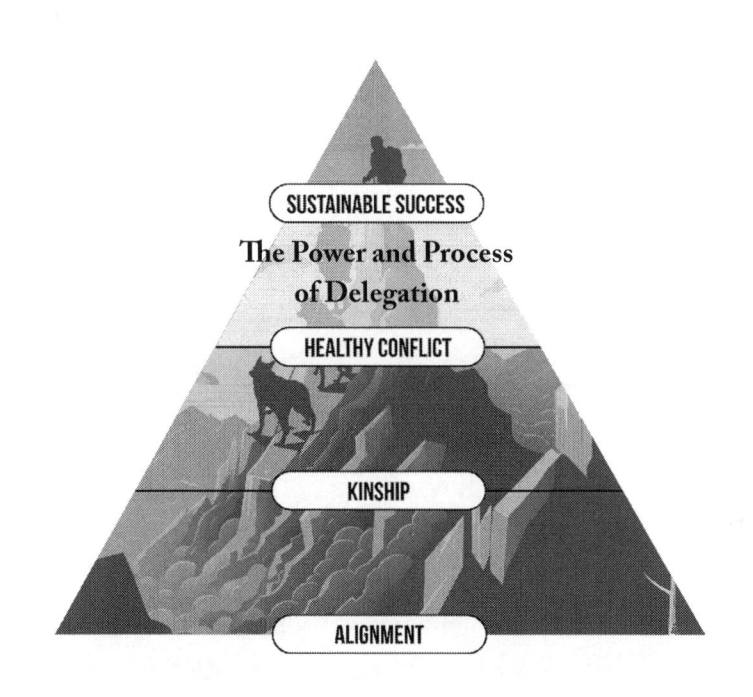

STEP 34 UP THE TRIBE TRIANGLE:

The Power and Process of Delegation

"Delegation is the power to build a vision and a legacy which is greater than yourself."
–Philip Folsom

We are here to make a difference, or, as Steve Jobs said; *to put a dent in the universe.* The size of that dent and how long it lasts, depends on how well we learn to delegate because nothing of significance was ever done alone. This one leadership skill will determine whether you can scale into significance or not.

> *"We accomplish all that we do through delegation*
> *-either through time or to other people."*
> Stephen R. Covey

To begin understanding how effective and sustainable delegation works, we must first understand the difference between leaders and managers. If you are reading this, then you are a leader, however you may also be both a leader *and* a manager at different times, with different people and on different projects. Both roles are indispensable for the long-term success of your projects and tribe.

The difference between leaders and managers is that leaders are people who can see and create a future that does not currently exist and managers are people who implement and maintain what currently exists. Both functions are necessary for the sustainable success of your team and they both support each other in symbiotic and reciprocal ways, however, to enact delegation effectively, you must be in the leadership role and understand the management capacity of whom you are delegating *to*.

The military has a clear delineation of these two organizational functions and how they interact. Officers are leaders and enlisted soldiers are managers. There are overlaps in both roles because there are officers whose job it is to manage and there are enlisted soldiers whose job is to lead but even those enlisted soldiers who lead are referred to as non-commissioned *officers*.

Putting up the flagpole

One of the best examples of delegation that I have ever heard of was one of the challenge questions on the promotion interview for officers in the army. The officer being interviewed was provided with a list of resources to install a flagpole.

These resources included a platoon of privates, a sergeant (a non-commissioned officer who both leads and manages the privates) and all the supplies required for the project including shovels, cement and other flagpole components. The challenge question to the officer was: as a leader, what is your first step in putting up the flagpole?

Most leaders today would view that challenge as a logistical exercise first and would begin that project with research into mixing cement, teaching the privates or reviewing project safety protocols. What would you do first as a leader needing a flagpole raised?

The correct answer is: *"Sergeant, put up the flagpole"*.

> *"Don't tell people how to do things, tell them what to do and let them surprise you with their results."*
> General George S. Patton

Your job as a leader is to see the need for a flagpole and initiate the installation of that mission. The ideal first step in that project is to delegate it to your sergeant or manager. If you step down into the management role on that project you step away from leading your team toward the next phase your shared vision. Leaders focus on strategy and managers focus on tactics. When you are pulled into tactical challenges you have surrendered strategy and this means surrendering vision.

If you find yourself regularly micromanaging people and projects it means you are struggling with surrendering control or have not found, or made, your sergeants.

"No one will make a great business who wants it all themselves or take all the credit."
–Andrew Carnegie

Finding and building sergeants

Leaders deal with vision and strategy. Managers deal with implementation and tactics. For a leader to be able to delegate and continue leading instead of managing, they need competent managers who have the ability to understand your vision and the ability to implement the mission. Finding and making these people is one of the greatest challenges of leaders in every arena throughout history. Those people are worth their weight in gold.

The only people you can effectively delegate to, understand and share your vision and have the competence to implement the missions that move your team toward it.

Vision is a deep understanding of the larger strategic purpose of the mission at hand. Have you made that vision crystal clear and do you have buy-in from your implementation team? Does your sergeant or manager have the mastery of skills, tools and process, to implement that shared mission? If your team does not have the ability to understand and implement your vision and mission you cannot successfully delegate.

Find or develop these people first before you can delegate or you will become an underperforming, disappointed and dysfunctional leader. You will find that the development of these people is more of your actual legacy than anything else you do as a Tribe Leader.

If you delegate projects and missions you will create an engaged team, but if you delegate authority you create *leaders* on your team. What you will never be able to delegate is *responsibility* because the ultimate responsibility is up to you in who, how and when you delegate. *Leadership consists of taking responsibility for everything that goes wrong and giving your subordinates credit for everything that goes right.*

Remember, appreciation and purpose is always the second paycheck for your sergeants and that acknowledgment is often worth more to them than the money. Pay that second paycheck early and often. Do not expect that to be reciprocal. Praise starts with leaders and rolls downhill.

> *"The art of delegation is one of the key skills any entrepreneur must master."*
> *–Richard Branson*

Tribe leaders must write and speak

Where are you being forced into micromanagement of projects that could, or should, be implemented by your team?

_____
_____
_____

What is the larger organizational cost of this? What could or should you be doing that would create larger, scalable results for your whole tribe?

_____
_____
_____

What is your delegation challenge?

_____
_____
_____

Your inability to surrender control?

_____
_____
_____

A lack of your team understanding the larger shared vision that the current mission serves?

_____
_____
_____

A lack of your team's mastery or competence in conducting the mission?

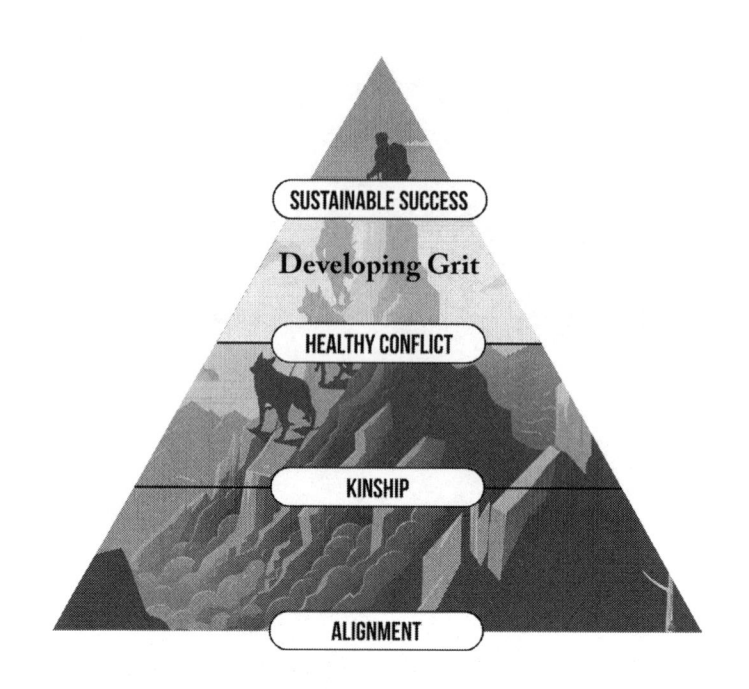

STEP 35 UP THE TRIBE TRIANGLE:

Developing Grit

"Embrace the suck."
–US Army Parable

Resiliency is the ability to recover from adversity. Grit is *applied resiliency* and the ability to *persevere* in the face of adversity. Grit is the stubborn refusal to quit. Without this ability to endure hardship, setbacks and defeat, your team will never be able to accomplish significant, meaningful things.

Grit is not innovative or sexy and it is not a sprint. It is consistently and relentlessly doing the *next right thing* that is required in the pursuit of your shared vision. Grit is moving forward when it is easier to stop or even retreat. Grit is long-term forward progress.

> *"Grit is living life like it's a marathon not a sprint."*
> *-Angela Duckworth*

Making and maintain grit

The American Psychological Association defines grit as a personality trait that is required for "the sustained interest in important long-term goals." These long-term goals are the shared vision we must continue to hold up like a lighthouse in the dark, because without that guiding light of purpose, grit will fade.

If your shared vision is not inspirational and aspirational, it will not produce the environment for grit. People will not persevere through suffering and sacrifice unless the challenge is deeply meaningful. Setting that passionate north star is your first and most important job, Tribe Leader.

> *"Grit is not just about stubborn persistence. It's also about choosing the right goals."*
> *-Angela Duckworth*

It is important to note that while grit is generated in the pursuit of meaningful goals, it is also generated by the honor-culture of kinship. Grit is rare and prolonged grit is heroic. Throughout history, this behavior is only found in the service of something or someone outside of ourselves. Without establishing the kinship level of the Tribe Triangle, you will not experience grit on your team.

Grit is made and no one is born with it, but like everything else in the Tribe Triangle, it can be cultivated. Grit is a rare expression of mental toughness and it is forged in a history of adversity, particularly doing the *right thing during adversity*. When we hold to our shared values when there are easier, less ethical routes available, we develop grit.

As a leader you must model this gritty behavior and take on the growth mindset of using challenges and adversity as opportunities to learn and get better instead of excuses to quit, or worse, compromise your values.

> *"True grit is making a decision and standing by it, doing what must be done."*
> *-John Wayne*

Challenges of grit

Grit grinds away at challenges blocking our path. It is the siege tactics that wear down adversaries. Birds gather and eat small stones that they use to help digest tough seeds and this is a good example of the positive use of grit but grit is also an abrasive force to everything it touches.

The violence inside engines also produces grit and that is the rough material that erodes moving parts. Grit must be intentionally directed in useful ways or it can become a toxic component in your relationships and culture. This is another reason that grit is included in the healthy conflict phase.

Grit is conflict and what grinds grain and adversity also destroys engines. Mindless, unintentional grit is the beginning stages of both hubris and martyrdom. When we see and feel the oil of morale become dark and clogged with grit, we must change it with compassion and self-care. Be mindful of when it is time to shift grit back into healthy resiliency.

Grit cannot be bought or forced. It is an example of long-term intrinsic motivation, commitment and a belief that what we are struggling toward is worth the effort. You deserve it. Your people and projects demand it.

Tribe leaders must write and speak.

What is a tough, long-term challenge that your team has repeatedly quit at or compromised standards? It may be a surrender of safety protocol, documentation, project preparation or follow up procedures.

_____

_____

_____

What is a tough, long-term personal challenge where you have repeatedly surrendered the field? Can you publicly own this and make a recommitment to model grit for your team?

_____

_____

_____

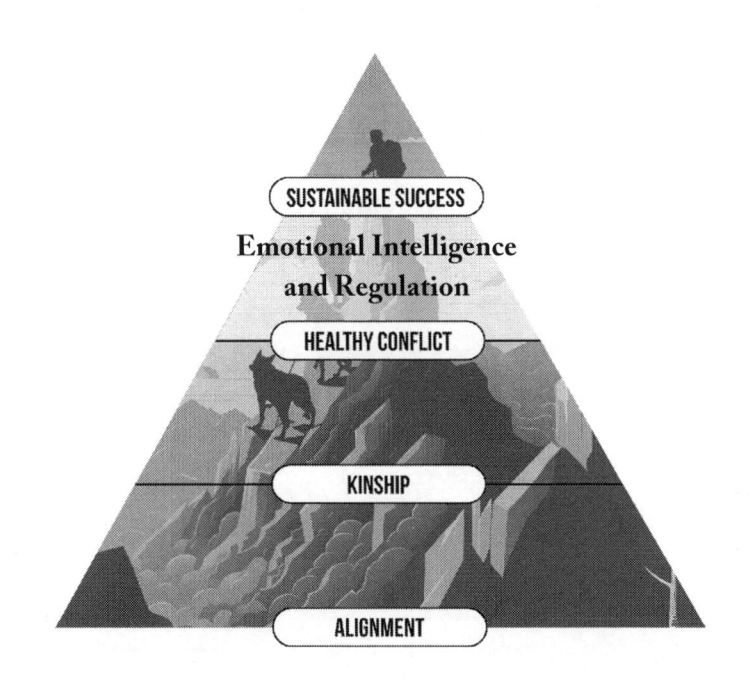

SUSTAINABLE SUCCESS
Emotional Intelligence and Regulation
HEALTHY CONFLICT
KINSHIP
ALIGNMENT

STEP 36 UP THE TRIBE TRIANGLE:

Emotional Intelligence and Regulation

IQ is a measure of intelligence.
EQ is the measure of success.

The reason why 'culture is king' is that regardless of your strategy, technology or marketing, at some point everything comes down to people and culture is the big bucket that contains all human behavior. At the bottom of every one of these buckets of human behaviors is a deep and messy layer of *emotions*.

Humans are inherently emotional beings and if you and your team do not have an understanding and skill in this universal and unavoidable human trait, you will not be sustainably successful. No business plan and no google search will provide the answers to the inevitable arrival of strong emotions. You must learn to look inward to understand and manage fear, defeat and other stress-related emotions.

"When a man is prey to his emotions, he is not his own master."
Spinoza

Emotions come first in every human experience. They happen microseconds before thoughts and thoughts are what dictate words, decisions and actions.

Emotions are the gauges on our human vehicle. They do not dictate our actions and are only symptoms of what is going on under the hood. This however, is indispensable information because if you do not know the status of your emotional state you will be underperforming, making poor choices and risk burnout and breakdown.

"The emotions of man are stirred more quickly than man's intelligence."
-Oscar Wilde

If we do not have control of our emotions, we are a slave to them. While it is true that we do not have control of the emotions that the experiences of defeat and conflict will generate, **we can develop control of** the thoughts that come next and the words, decisions and actions that follow.

If you haven't developed the self-awareness and skills to manage your emotions you will struggle with empathy, defeat and everything else involved in all significant struggles of life. Without emotional intelligence and emotional regulation you will not get far and neither will your team. As Tribe leader, you are the lighthouse that your team looks to when things get stormy and conflict arises like it always does. Emotional regulation practice is the rock that your lighthouse is built on.

Anyone or anything that can manipulate your emotions becomes your master. **Never make a permanent decision based on a temporary emotion.**

> *"Between stimulus and response, there is a space. In that space lies our freedom and power to choose our response. In our response lies our growth and freedom."*
> *Viktor Frankl*

Human emotions are messy, mysterious and unavoidable things and for most of the history of corporate culture they not been successfully addressed. Even the term 'Human Resources' reflects the idea that people are just company assets or supplies to be managed. This philosophy of considering people as simply *resources* has led to a great dissatisfaction in the corporate world and unfathomable loss of engagement, commitment and feelings of belonging. All of that degrades performance. People *feel* things and that cannot be ignored or disregarded.

You will notice that when we greet each other, it always involves some form of "how are you doing" or "how are you feeling"? This alone should give us an idea of how important feelings and emotions are. The fact that we never give or expect an authentic answer should also give us an idea of how poorly most pride-based cultures are in dealing with real emotions.

"To be successful we must learn to navigate the messy parts of life."
-Joshua Wenner

Emotional intelligence is the language of kinship. Emotional regulation is the applied resiliency that is required for your team to navigate all forms of healthy conflict and persevere through adversity. These core human skills are the ability to manage both your own emotions as well as understand the emotions of the people in your family and work team.

Like everything else in leadership, emotional intelligence and regulation begins with self-awareness. If you are not conscious of your own emotional state you will not only make poor, emotionally-driven decisions which will degrade your relationships and projects but you will also model a lack of stability. This is crippling for your leadership and your team.

You must develop emotional intelligence and regulation in order to face failures and learn from them. This is central to every aspect of success in healthy conflict.

Responsibility is the ability to respond instead of react. The ability to respond is only available if we are emotionally regulated. Strong negative emotions such as anger, sadness, anxiety and hopelessness force us into playing defense instead of offense. We become risk adverse and our choices narrow to the safe choices that limit risk but also potential.

Fear, or some form of that emotion, will be your constant companion during the Healthy Conflict phase of the Tribe Triangle. All challenges create more negative and prolonged emotions. Be prepared for fear: fear of success, fear of failure, fear of inadequacy and fear of abandonment. *Those fears and doubts are contagious and have ended more projects and dreams than defeat could ever dream of. Experiencing fear is not a choice but responding to fear with courage, is.*

> *"Emotional regulation flows naturally from being in the presence of someone we trust"*
> *–Bonnie Badenoch*

Emotions are real and powerful things but they do not actually exist anywhere except in our mind and nervous system. Use them for what they are; gauges that let us know what our human experience is but do not let them be the force that drives the decisions and actions that *could be*.

If we are able to gain some experience with normalizing the healthy acknowledgment and expression of emotions, we will be healthier and higher performing humans. This invaluable knowledge of emotional awareness and regulation will elevate all aspects of kinship including your resiliency, morale and feelings of belonging. An increase in kinship will cascade into increased levels of performance in every component of the Healthy Conflict phase of your team's journey up the Tribe Triangle.

> *"Everything can be taken from a man but one thing: the last of the human freedoms–to choose one's attitude in any given set of circumstances, to choose one's own way."*
> *Viktor Frankl*

Remember, people don't leave jobs, they leave bad bosses. Bad bosses don't choose to be bad; they are just emotionally unregulated people.

> *"We are dangerous when we are not conscious of our responsibility for how we behave, think and feel."*
> *–Marshall Rosenberg*

Tribe leaders must write and speak

How often do you authentically share what you are feeling or hear what your family or team members are feeling? This can be scary and triggering but you and your team will get better at it!

_____
_____
_____

When and where is the ideal time for this sharing of emotions with your people and projects?

_____
_____
_____

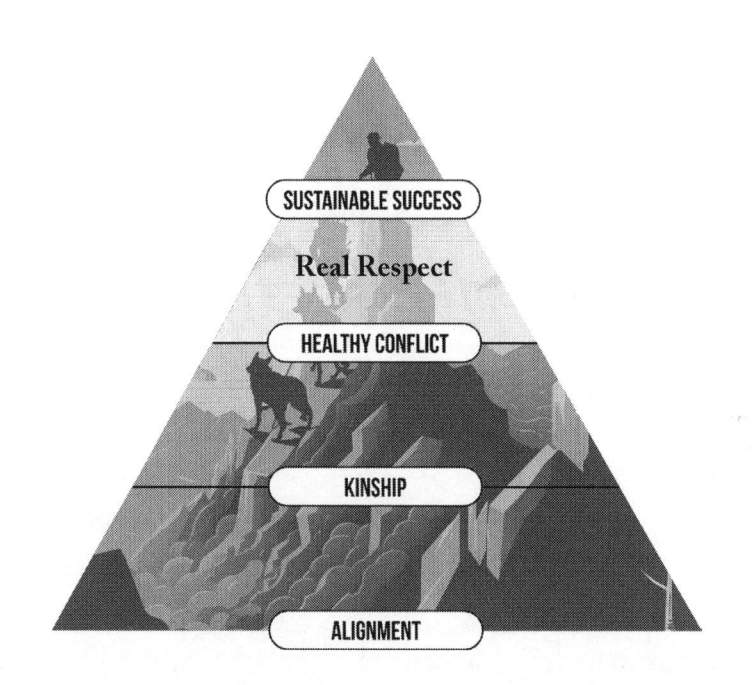

STEP 37 UP THE TRIBE TRIANGLE:

Real Respect

Real Respect is Applied Kinship.

Respect is an often-misunderstood component of modern society where people consider respect a *right* instead of a valuable earned level of kinship. This diminished version of respect is more like politeness than genuine respect which is defined as *'a feeling of deep admiration for someone elicited by their abilities, qualities or achievements'*. Genuine respect is an expression of *value*.

Politeness is granted, respect is *earned*

Respect is eared through behavior during shared adversity and this only truly happens during the healthy conflict phase of the Tribe Triangle.

During the alignment phase we learn about our team's culture and this develops knowledge and appreciation. During the kinship phase we learn about our team's people and this brings us closer relationships and the experience of belonging. During the healthy conflict phase, we learn about our team's character and this brings us respect. Families and organizations with high amounts of mutual respect demonstrate a higher level of overall success including increased morale, engagement and productivity. **Adversity does not build character it reveals it.**

"Knowledge will give you power, but character respect."
–Bruce Lee

Respectful behavior during conflict generates respect. We learn and reveal more about ourselves during failure and adversity than we do during success. This includes the unavoidable internal conflict within a competitive and ambitious team as well as the external conflict with competitors whom we must strive against. Respect is reciprocal because when it is earned it must be returned.

You cannot decree respect on your team, you can only behave

respectfully and model the way you carry responsibility. Similarly, you cannot force people to respect you but you can refuse to be disrespected. Disrespect on a team is evidence of a culture failure in either alignment or kinship. As a leader, you must be vigilant for actions or feelings of disrespect on your team.

> *"Whoever acts with respect will get respect."*
> *-Rumi*

Genuine respect involves a healthy component of recognition and regard of power. This does not mean fear but there must be an acknowledgement that there are consequences to disrespect and you must have access to these healthy responses. **We teach people how to treat us.**

Dangerous tools like saws, knives or stoves are an example of this form of respect. They are very powerful tools but that power is drawn directly from the ability to cut or burn which is useful and necessary to be valuable but when treated without respect can cause injury. Powerful tools and people are dangerous tools and people and must be respected.

Often, experiences of disrespect can stem from lack of communication style awareness and application. This indispensable kinship skill is vital for making and maintaining respect in your family and work team. Many times, what is construed as disrespect is simply an unskillful communication.

Lingering feelings and expressions of disrespect can also stem from feeling threatened by a family or team member becoming more powerful when you are not or getting promoted and praised when you are not. This is an example of lack of alignment and when you see this unhealthy lack of respect coming from competition in your family or team, you must quickly shore up and recommit to your culture foundation of shared vision, values and mission. When one of us wins, we all win. This is true respect and another reason why making and maintaining genuine respect can only happen in the healthy conflict phase.

Do not mistake respect for awe or deference. Be vigilant of this behavior from yourself toward those you admire and be extra watchful for this in your subordinate's treatment of you. This false sense of respect is toxic and will undo your kinship culture which requires the safety to disagree and fail.

This false sense of respect is driven by pride and leads to ignorance and hubris.
"Unthinking respect for authority is the greatest enemy of truth."
-Albert Einstein

Like everything else on this journey up the Tribe Triangle, respect starts with you, Tribe Leader. Respecting yourself leads to both self-discipline and self-care.

Respect is both earned and lost. Respect must be constantly maintained and is a driver of harmony in your family and team. The harmony of mutual respect is never permanent and there is no stasis or balance in the world especially in families and business. It is everchanging and, at its best, there is a harmony and respect during healthy conflict and change.

Mutual respect is the foundation of genuine harmony."
-Dali Lama

Tribe leaders must write and speak

Who is the most respected member of your family or team? What behavior over time created that respect?

_____

_____

_____

Who is the least respected member of your family or team? What behavior over time created that lack of respect?

_____

_____

_____

STEP 38 UP THE TRIBE TRIANGLE:

Stretch Goals and Failure

"If at first you succeed, try something harder."

Stretch goals are inspiring and ambitious targets that are so challenging they exceed our current known ability to complete. In fact, stretch goals aren't meant to be fully completed, they are meant to stretch us.

When was the last time you failed at something you fully committed to? To answer this honestly (and Tribe Leaders are honest, especially with themselves) you must first ask yourself when was the last time you *fully committed* to something?

Most of us keep something in reserve. This leaves a psychological escape hatch or backdoor where we can run to when things get hard and the potential for defeat arrives. By staying uncommitted we can always tell ourselves that 'when we finally commit, things will be different'. This is an adolescent strategy of avoiding failure and leads us to only commit one foot in relationships and projects. Ironically, this failure-avoidance strategy often leads directly to the failure we are avoiding.

At Google and many other high performing organizations, they have addressed this universal human defect of avoiding failure through lack of commitment by *building failure into their goal-setting strategy*. They expect a certain amount of failure from every goal. If a goal is completely met it wasn't big enough. If you are always hitting your goals, how can you ever know how much potential is left on the table?

> *"A goal is not always meant to be reached.*
> *It often serves simply as something to aim at."*
> *–Bruce Lee*

The only way to find your edges are to go past them. Experiencing failure is the cost of exploring potential. In addition, experiencing failure is how we learn and expand capacity and skill so the next goal-setting sequence is even bigger.

Normalizing failure in the pursuit of stretch goals is the most effective growth strategy available to you and your family or team but it requires the trust, safety and resiliency of kinship to sustain. Failure is damaging to our psychology but growth is healing to our psychology. Stretch goals will stretch you and your team.

> *"What you get by achieving your goals is not as important as what you become by achieving your goals."*
> *-Henry David Thoreau*

Easy goals will be achievable and less challenging but will generate little genuine excitement and lead to no breakthroughs. Stretch goals will contain the potential for failure but also inspiration and growth as well as breakthroughs. This is where freedom and meaning exist.

The capacity and character increase from stretch goals is often more important than the goal itself. The process of commitment, failure and learning is indispensable for sustainable success. Stretch goals are the road toward what is possible in life. That road is more important than the goals along the road.

> *"A goal should scare you a little and excite you a lot."*
> *-Joe Vitale*

Stretch goals are obvious in the realm of exercise. Besides requiring you to stretch to be healthy, goals only achieve results if they are slightly beyond your limits. In weightlifting it means periodically going to failure which is where the maximum growth happens.

The exercise example is also important because it includes the fact that we do not get stronger *during* the challenge. We get stronger in the recovery phase *afterwards*. The same is true for every stretch goal in every arena of your life. Whether it be a relationship or a challenging project, we only get stronger and gain more capacity in the recovery and learning afterwards.

This recovery phase is the reflection and recovery we must do afterwards to reap the benefits of the struggle. This will often include forgiveness to yourself, your family and team.

Setting goals is how we make the invisible visible. Setting stretch goals is how we transform potential into the palpable and real. There are two primary factors to consider if your team is ready to tackle the opportunity and challenge of engaging with stretch goals.

First, are you currently successful at hitting your standard goals? Are you generally winning in the arena in which you play? This confidence and feeling of being successful is vital before we take on the 'failure' that is inherent when engaging with stretch goals.

If you have any doubt about the level of morale and optimism on your team, you should have an authentic conversation with them about whether or not to implement stretch goals because they require full participation and engagement for the character and capacity stretch to be successful.

Secondly, are there resources not being utilized in your family or work team? Is there a surplus of time that is available or could be *made* available by cutting out redundant meetings or time suck activities like doom scrolling on social media?

Is there a surplus of money that is being spent on frivolous, non-essential costs that could be better used with a more valuable and inspiring stretch goal project?

Are your people underutilized and needing more responsibility and challenge?

If you are on a winning streak and have capacity that could be better used, you are in the perfect, healthy conflict position to take advantage of stretch goals.

Tribe leaders must write and speak

Is morale, inspiration and competitiveness lacking in your family or work team? Is the personal and professional growth flatlined or stagnant? Where is this happening?

_____

_____

_____

Does your team have the resiliency and capacity to engage with stretch goals?

_____

_____

_____

SUSTAINABLE SUCCESS

Taking Off the Armor and Coming Home

HEALTHY CONFLICT

KINSHIP

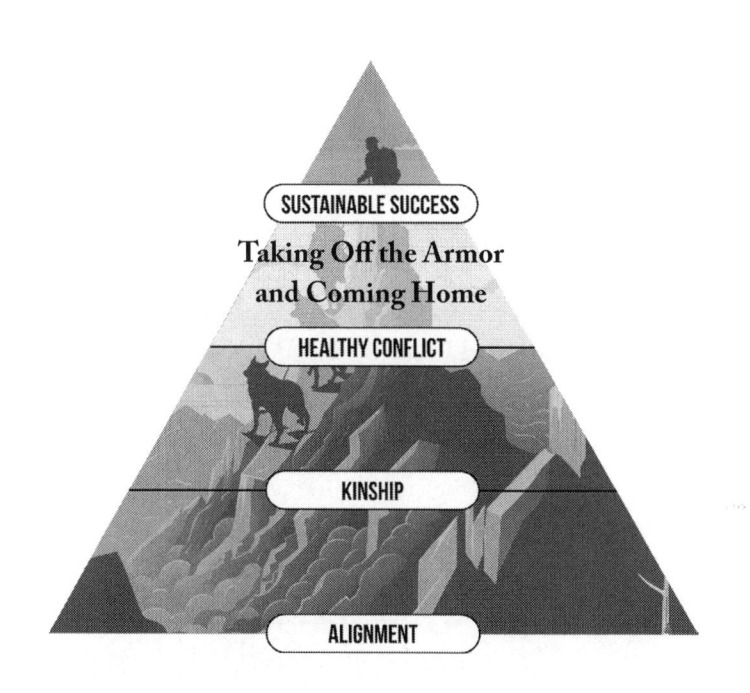

ALIGNMENT

STEP 39 UP THE TRIBE TRIANGLE:

Taking Off the Armor and Returning Home

"Take off the armor; dare to be vulnerable,
dare to unwrap yourself and dare yourself to be yourself."
–Maria Shriver

The Healthy Conflict phase of the Tribe Triangle is a full commitment to entering the arena of life instead of waiting for some external permission or validation. Whether this is your family relationships, fitness journey or competition in business, this experience is accepting that there will be setbacks, friction and defeats. These hurt.

To enter and survive in the full arena of life we must put on some sort of armor. We explored and discovered versions of this armor in the chapters on Grit, Accountability and Change Management. **Kinship is where we built the armor and Healthy Conflict is where we wear it.**

For those of us who played team sports or experienced some other form of honor-based culture like the military or first response community, we know that armor well. The armor stops emotions and thoughts from stopping our mission. Tough times create tough people.

Without that personal and cultural armor, we will be psychologically and professionally wounded and our journey will end. We cannot successfully and sustainably compete without that armor. Armor limits feeling. This is valuable but also dangerous, especially if we don't know how or when to take it off.

When we become gritty and successful people instead of people who are gritty and successful, we have adopted an *identity*. An identity is a way of being that we adopt that does not require struggle to maintain. It is habitual. This is efficient but also removes the ability to grow and adapt. When we adopt an identity of grittiness that is required to compete and survive during struggle, we also become less sensitive, less vulnerable and less empathetic.

These leadership skills and tools are vital for living a holistically successful life which requires us to be deeply connected to events and relationships. Transitioning from the struggle of the arena back home is an age-old challenge for the professional.

All athletes and soldiers transitioning from their professional life which defines them, back into the civilian world, know this experience well. Professional athletes play hurt and professional soldiers fight wounded. They can do this because they have embodied the warrior ethos and adopted that warrior identity. To be able to operate at that level in those arenas they have built and put on armor. To be a successful Tribe Leader in the Healthy Conflict phase of your journey, you have too.

Are you an entrepreneur who forges ahead in the face of setback after setback?

Are you a parent relentlessly facing family challenges without quitting?

Are you a manager of a challenging team or in a challenging industry who cannot afford to be vulnerable? If so, you are wearing armor.

> *"A man who is putting on his armor to go to war should not boast like a man who is taking it off."*
> *–African Proverb and Bible*

The challenge with adopting the identity of the thick-skinned, armor-wearing realist, is that we must be aware of the times, places and people where the armor is no longer required. We also must know how to take it off.

Are you being strong or are you only numb?

Some of the symptoms of wearing armor in environments where we do not need it is a loss of vitality and passion. Are you actively enjoying sunsets, food and children? Are you filled with active gratitude and are you feeling compassion for yourself and others? Do you laugh and cry? Are the activities that you once found engaging and pleasurable have become unfulfilling? Are you struggling with addictions or coping mechanisms to function in social settings? Is your sleep suffering?

> *"To love, we must remove our armor, exposing our heart.*
> *For love cannot be had without the risk of being wounded."*
> *-John Mark Green*

There are a host of best practices for the vital transition from struggle to vulnerability. Some of the best practices are battle-tested reintegration rituals from warrior cultures of every era.

When it was time to come home, the medieval knights would ritually take off their armor and weapons. This would usually happen in the church where the battle-weary warrior would say the rosary and walk the church labyrinth in only a robe. These knights would also engage with intentionally vulnerable and humble acts such as pilgrimages and writing love letters.

The samurai from medieval Japan had similar reintegration rituals that included engaging in the inherently peaceful acts of calligraphy, pottery and flower arranging.

Establish your own reintegration ritual so when you return home from the challenges of your day, you can take off your armor and reconnect with the fullness of your life. Walk the dog, take your shoes off and walk on the earth. Purify yourself from the debris of your battles with a shower. Turn off your phone and don't check your email until tomorrow. Somehow the world will continue to turn without you managing it.

> *"How do people like us take off our armor? One piece at a time."*
> *-Holly Black*

We need to learn to understand and behave without the reference point of our own power and security. If we don't, we will lose connection from our people and the purpose of our vision as well as ourselves. You deserve this. Your people and projects demand it.

Tribe leaders must write and speak

What is the armor you put on to survive the challenges of your day? When do you have to 'not care about what people think about you'? When do you 'soldier on' when inside you are scared, insecure or disappointed?

_____

_____

_____

What is a reintegration ritual that you will enact after work so you don't bring the battle home?

_____

_____

_____

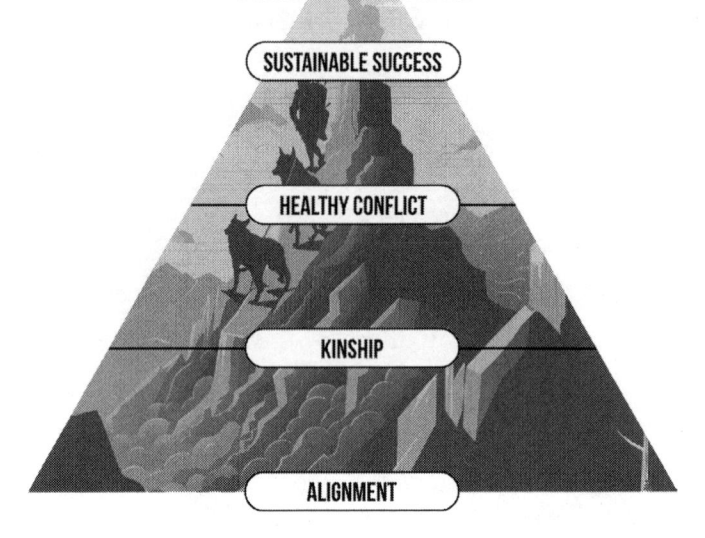

Sustainable Success

- SUSTAINABLE SUCCESS
- HEALTHY CONFLICT
- KINSHIP
- ALIGNMENT

PHASE 4 UP THE TRIBE TRIANGLE:

Introduction to the Sustainable Success level of the Tribe Triangle

"The wolf on the hill is not as hungry as the wolf climbing the hill."
–Arnold Schwarzenegger

Success is a universal goal for every person, family and organization. Many never get there and those that do rarely stay. Only 53 companies that were on the Fortune 500 in 1955 are still there. National sports teams almost never repeat and the few sports teams that have won 3 in a row are legendary. These teams are so rare we have a special name for them, dynasties. It is important to note that this is the same word we use to describe families that are so sustainably successful and rare that we reserve that term for them.

Becoming successful with your family and team is worth celebrating (which is one of the 13 steps of the Sustainable Success level of the Tribe Triangle) but even better than becoming successful is *staying successful*. The ability to stay successful over time requires all the work you have been doing in addition to a specific strategy and skill set that enables you to maintain what you have made. These are the 13 primary tools you will need to navigate the rare air of sustainable success:

1. Maintaining flow state
2. Vitality
3. Great leaders don't create success they create leaders
4. Honesty and self-reflection, the mirror
5. External coaching
6. Celebration and traditions
7. Mentorship and Training
8. Vulnerability
9. Service and self-sacrifice
10. Freedom and meaning
11. Being a professional
12. Reconnection and Recommitment
13. Legacy of reclaiming kinship

This level of your journey up the Tribe Triangle will be the true test of your leadership with your people and more importantly your leadership with yourself. It will be the most challenging and rewarding experience of your life. You deserve it. Your legacy demands it.

You gotta' be hungry to hunt.

Making and Mantaining Flow State

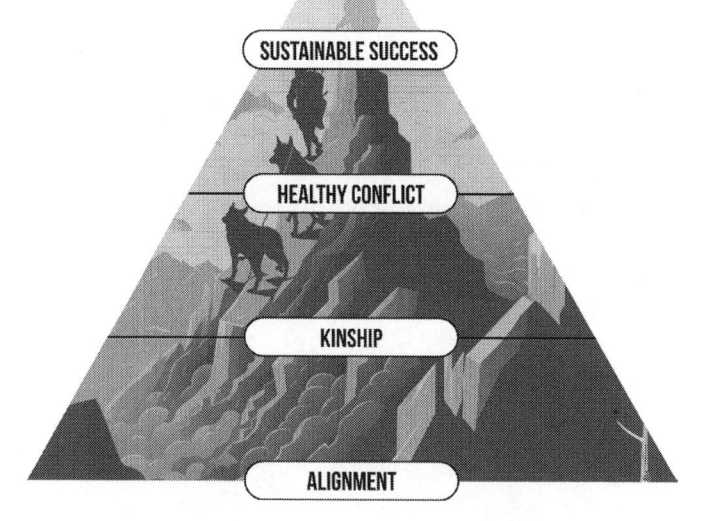

- SUSTAINABLE SUCCESS
- HEALTHY CONFLICT
- KINSHIP
- ALIGNMENT

STEP 40 UP THE TRIBE TRIANGLE:

Making and Maintaining Flow State

"Those who flow as life flows know they need no other force."

Lao Tzu

Flow state is a term from sports psychology that refers to the behavior of an athlete who is operating at peak performance. The same state can exist in every aspect of our lives including relationships and business.

Flow state is an experience of full engagement in the process. Time passes quickly when we are in flow state and even though we may be immersed in epic challenges, they are more successful, creative and enjoyable than usual. New solutions to old problems appear and synergy between people and ideas arise as if by magic. Flow state is an experience of energy, focus and high performance. It is not magic or a mystery. The high growth and accomplishment of flow state can be created and maintained.

> *"The way you learn the most is when you are doing something with such enjoyment that you don't notice that the time passes."*
> *-Albert Einstein*

Flow state is understood and reproducible. Flow consists of six primary neurochemicals which include norepinephrine, dopamine, endorphins, anandamide, oxytocin and serotonin. These chemicals are released during certain activities that are connected to the pursuit of challenging and meaningful goals. This set of six chemicals creates an experience of genuine well-being as well as high performance. Flow state is so fulfilling that people who have accessed it report it as being a high point in their life.

> *"Flow is more than an optimal state of consciousness, one where we feel our best and perform our best. It also appears to be the one practical answer to the question: What is the meaning of life? Flow is what makes life worth meaning."*
> *Steven Kotler*

Flow state happens when the challenges we are facing are large enough they require our full attention but are not too big that they lead to doubt and indecisiveness. Managing that sweet spot for all the members of your family or team is one of the most common and ongoing challenges of leadership. Undertaking those challenges is well worth it because flow state not only increases the quality of life for your people but the quantity of success you can create in your organization.

> *"The happiest people spend much of their time in a state of flow-the state in which people are so involved in an activity that nothing else seems to matter; the experience itself is so enjoyable that people will do it even at great cost, for the sheer sake of doing it."*
> *–Mihaly Csikszentmihalyi*

Challenges of making and maintaining flow state

Experiences of being overwhelmed or 'in over your head' lead to anxiety and loss of flow. These feelings come from projects or processes that are beyond the scope of your team or simply unfamiliar. If you feel or notice anxiety, dread and stress in yourself or your team, you are experiencing the signs of overwhelm that will inhibit flow state and peak performance.

The other side of that stress continuum is when people are underutilized and underchallenged. This will appear as symptoms of diversions such as social media scrolling, gossip and other forms of distraction and lack of engagement. Underutilized and underchallenged people will often be looking for larger, more meaningful challenges, teams and careers. Retention is a function of regular flow state.

Uninspired challenges lead to boredom and loss of flow. Flow state is not relaxed, it is highly energized. People need to care deeply about the challenge at hand for flow state to be possible. In addition, these challenges need to be inspiring and meaningful. One of the primary drivers of this is regular and repeated recommitment to the shared aspirational vision for the future that you and your team are heading towards. Flow state is the experience of being pulled toward that future vision yet simultaneously being fulfilled by the current process.

Flow state is both a product and result of focusing on a single, challenging activity that is both engaging and meaningful. Multi-tasking disables flow. Splitting your brain processing power across multiple challenges slows your decisions and actions down by 40%. To make and maintain flow we need to limit distractions by turning off notifications and anything else that diffuses focus.

Drivers of making and maintaining flow state

Write down your perfect day. As adults in this era of humanity, we all know what we should be doing and what we shouldn't if we are living our perfect day. Things we should not be doing cause a loss of energy, vitality and focus. For most people this includes too much screen time, junk food and other low energy producing behavior.

Activities we should be doing contribute flow energy to our day. These positive practices include meditation, nature, exercise and optimized sleep. Make that list and write it down. The closer we can hew to that perfect day, the more flow state opportunities we open up and the longer those states will last. This is a hard path to follow but the harder you work the more flow you achieve and flow is when life feels effortless. Flow is the feeling of overcoming resistance.

Flow state is both a result and contributor to confidence. We must have the skills to match the challenges that we face to be in flow. To face a challenge that is significant enough to warrant our full, flow state engagement we will need to have the mastery to match it. This can only come from battle-tested repetitions over time which is why regular flow state with your family or team only happens later in your culture development journey.

We can augment the potential and duration of flow by working around other aligned people in an active kinship community. Energy is either being gathered or lost by our life protocol and community. Either way, that energy is flowing. You can direct this flow by skillful leadership. People in flow state describe the sensation as instinctive and the experience of knowing what will happen next. We can nudge this forward by focusing on the process or journey instead of the outcome or destination. Vision big. Work small.

> *"I entered a flow state. I've been there before while climbing.*
> *You are not thinking ahead.*
> *You are just thinking about what is in front of you each second.'*
> *–Aaron Ralston, Professional Climber*

Tribe leaders must write and speak

What are 3 things you know you should not be doing in your day that distract you from flow state?

_____

_____

_____

What are 3 lifestyle practices that increase your vitality and flow?

_____

_____

_____

Where is your team either overwhelmed by too large of a challenge or unengaged because the challenge is too small and uninspiring?

_____

_____

_____

Growing Vitality

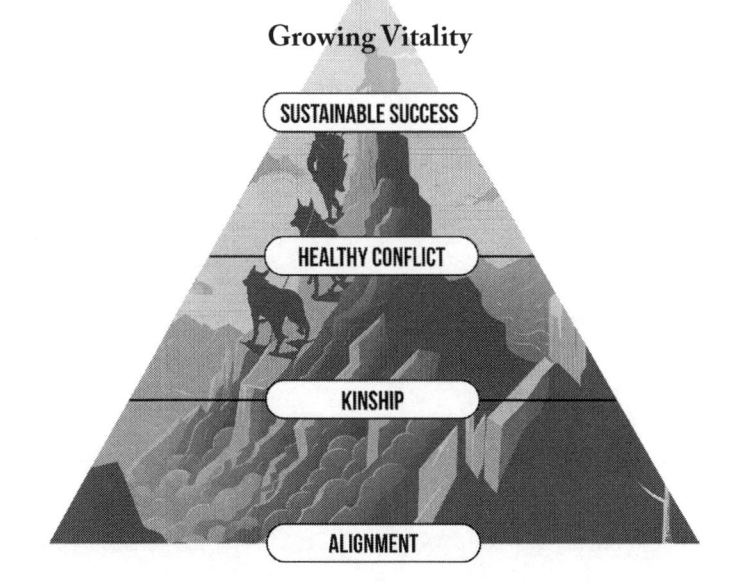

- SUSTAINABLE SUCCESS
- HEALTHY CONFLICT
- KINSHIP
- ALIGNMENT

STEP 41 UP THE TRIBE TRIANGLE:

Growing Vitality

"The chief condition on which life, health and vigor depends on is action. It is by action that an organism develops its faculties, increases its energy and attains the fulfillment of its destiny."
–Colin Powell

Vitality is life force, eagerness and passion. It is defined as 'the ability to live and develop' as well as 'physical or mental vigor especially when highly developed'.

Vitality can be developed and is a product of resiliency, grit and all the other steps of your culture development journey. It is the one true measure of the efficacy of your people, your process and your culture. A job or family without vitality is a river without water.

Success is the top of the mountain. To make that success sustainable, we are going to have to explore and implement vitality best practices because getting to the top of any mountain in your life is not nearly as hard as staying there. The ability to not just *arrive* but to *thrive* is a matter of vitality.

Vitality is a direct product of the first three levels of the Tribe Triangle. If you or your people are struggling with burnout or lack of motivation it is a sign that you need to go back and shore up one of those levels.

Vitality of Alignment

Vitality is much more than pleasure, ease or happiness. Vitality is the vigor and drive that imbues your people to seek greatness, freedom and meaning as well as the ability to persevere through the unavoidable adversity involved in everything great. All of these sources of greatness come from the three pillars of culture alignment.

Your shared aspirational **vision** is a primary source of inspiration and vitality. People need to believe that freedom and meaning is possible and that their days and their work is significant. Without an aspirational vision both you and your people will hemorrhage vitality and collapse into distraction, resentment and nihilism which is the condition of no vitality.

A grandiose vision will quickly fade without the **shared values** that create a pathway toward it. These values are the commandments that guide travelers through the desert toward your promised land. Again, like everything else in your family and team, you must model these values.

Your *shared missions* are also an indispensable component to vitality. The transparency, collaboration and reciprocity involved in shared missions are huge drivers of vitality because people are compelled to participate when their participation is seen and valued. Even seemingly simple shared tasks can be vitality drivers when people feel genuinely important and involved.

> *"Enthusiasm is that ingredient of vitality mixed with a firm belief in what you are doing that ensures the success of any project you undertake."*
> *-Dale Carnegie*

Vitality of Kinship

Vitality is the life force in people and organizations and there are no dead or dull families, careers or companies, only unvital ones.

The ongoing Harvard Study of Adult Development is the longest lasting, most comprehensive study in history. Started in 1938, that study discovered that the number one source of health, happiness and overall vitality is close, vital relationships.

Looking back at the Kinship level of your journey up the Tribe Triangle you will discover you have access to all the levers of relationship vitality. Have you recommitted to building and maintaining close friendships at work? Have you become skillful at using the different communication styles and the platinum rule? These are all sources of vitality that come from your people.

> *"Vitality is a way of being eager and engaged. This ethos is built by your culture and passed on by the behavior of your people."*
> *-T.S. Eliot*

Vitality of Healthy Conflict

There is a commonly held misbelief that we get strong in the gym. We do not. We get strong in the recovery period *after* the challenges of the gym when our muscles heal with more capacity and size. The same dynamic holds true in every aspect of your life from relationship conflict to business competition. Vitality is a function of recovery and this needs to be acknowledged and normalized.

In every aspect of the Healthy Conflict phase there is an opportunity for vitality but only if we accept the need for failure and recovery. Can your people ask for help and delegate when needed? Have they accepted setbacks as a normal part of competition, innovation and accountability? Have you introduced and modeled the self-care of emotional regulation and recovery? These are all indispensable components of vitality.

"You may encounter many defeats, but you must not be defeated. In fact, the encountering may be the very experience which creates the vitality and the power to endure."
–Maya Angelou

Vitality is passion and may be the most important resource you manage, Tribe Leader. Vitality is the energy to live and work meaningfully and do significant things. Nurturing and investing in the development of vitality returns the dividend of living fully.

Everything we do and do not do either adds to our vitality and energy or takes away from it. When you have vitality in your family or work team you will see and feel your people come alive as though all their switches have been turned on. Highly vital people are eager. For this to happen you must be eager.

*"Live a vital life. If you live well, you will earn well.
If you live well, it will show in your face. There will be something
unique and magical about you if you live well. It will infuse
not only your personal life but also your business.
And it will give you a vitality nothing else can give."
–Jim Rohn*

Tribe leaders must write and speak

Where do you see and feel apathy in your family and team? This dullness is a symptom of a lack of vitality.

_____

_____

_____

Have your people lost commitment to your shared vision, values and mission? How and when will you recommit to your foundation of alignment?

_____

_____

_____

Have your people lost connection to the vitality between each other? How and when will you reconnect to the drivers of kinship?

_____

_____

_____

**Leaders Create
More Leaders**

(SUSTAINABLE SUCCESS)

(HEALTHY CONFLICT)

(KINSHIP)

(ALIGNMENT)

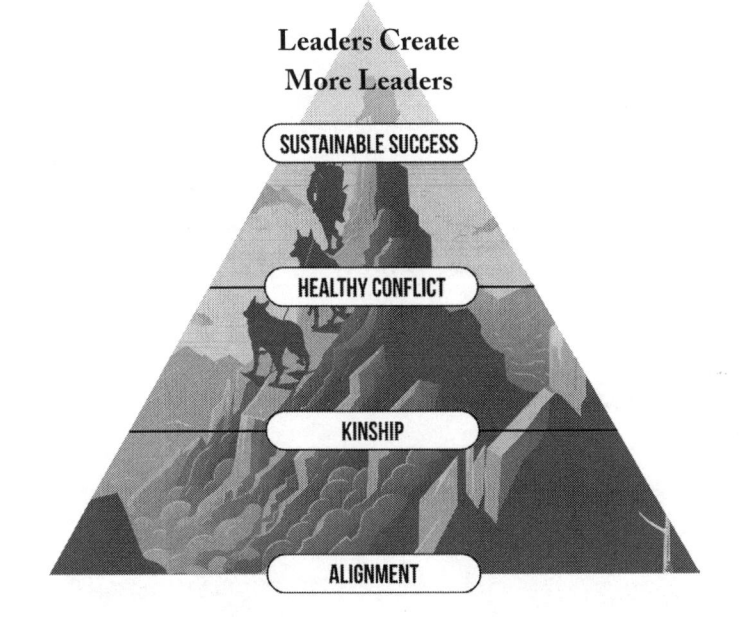

STEP 42 UP THE TRIBE TRIANGLE:

Leaders Create Leaders

"Leaders don't create followers, they create more leaders."
−Tom Peters

We are experiencing an evolution of leadership. The top down, authoritarian leadership model of central control is dead. If you are still trying to implement this with your family and work team, your sustainable success will be dead too. That outdated model was killed by the ever-accelerating rate of change which demands the active participation in the innovative worldview of autonomous leaders.

This new reality was initially discovered and implemented in the military that noticed the unpredictable and lightning-fast tactics of insurgents dismantling the old central control culture of the military which was too slow to respond effectively to rapidly changing battlefields. This awareness led to driving autonomy down to the lowest level possible. This meant empowering soldiers to make immediate decisions in the actual battlefield where the action is actually happening instead of waiting for directions from a distant and remote leadership structure.

> *"Great leaders create movements empowering the tribe to communicate. They establish the foundation for people to make connections, as opposed to commanding people to follow them."*
> *–Seth Godin*

Big corporations are faced with the same challenges in today's world of fast changing technology and information. This is why big companies lose the small battles that become big movements. The companies that adopt the most empowering leadership structure with the most autonomous leaders at every level win.

> *"Evolution is not survival of the fittest. It is survival of the most adaptable."*
> *–Philip Folsom*

Leadership skills used to be a valuable but optional trait of individuals, families and work teams. Leadership skills are now mandatory for both surviving and thriving. Leaders are the ones that see a vision for the future that does not exist. They are also the people with the ability to take risks and decisive actions to move projects and procedures toward that future. That future will contain challenges and opportunities appearing on the horizon at an ever-increasing rate. Creating leaders is a survival strategy.

Creating leaders is valuable and has a price. Here's how to pay it.

Responsibility is the ability to respond. Leaders have this, however, like everything at this stage of the Tribe Triangle there is a cost required.

Leaders are the people willing to take on the heavy burden of authority and accountability to make decisions as well as the burden of mistakes. Mistakes will be made and unless you have established a culture of resiliency and grit, leaders will not appear. If you are not seeing your people regularly stepping up into leadership, review the chapters on resiliency, risk-taking and grit and recommit to the work there. You will see transformation.

The ability to create more leaders on your team will involve risk and conflict. Leaders make decisions and these decisions will affect other people, projects and procedures. Some of these decisions will fail. Until you have established your Healthy Conflict level of the Tribe Triangle you will struggle with people stepping up into leadership. Continually encouraging risk and accepting failure will make it safe for your people to step into their leadership potential.

"The manager accepts the status quo; the leader challenges it."
-Warren Bennis

Transparently celebrating your successes and admitting your own mistakes will normalize the opportunities and challenges that come with leadership. This will also reinforce the fact that leadership development is ongoing and no one is perfect.

Your legacy as a leader will not be what you accomplish. It will be the leaders you create.

Empowering your people to claim their intrinsically motivated sovereignty is the magic bullet for ongoing engagement and overall performance. Everyone has talent and everyone has ambition. Can you unlock it?

"Leaders create and inspire new leaders by instilling faith in their leadership abilities and helping them develop and hone leadership skills they don't know they possess."
John C. Maxwell

More and more, today's contemporary workforce wants to be part of the decision-making that creates results. People want to be able to express themselves and be active participants in moving toward meaningful and significant things. Active involvement in meaningful, purposeful projects is in the top of young professional's demands for commitment to a company.

Nurture the inherent leadership in every member of your team. We can draw this out by our direct engagement with these people. Remember, appreciation is a form of paycheck that you have an unlimited amount of. Use it. Recognizing the leadership traits and behaviors of your people will accelerate their leadership development and has a tremendous culture and performance return on investment.

> *"Leadership is not defined by the exercise of power but the capacity to increase the sense of power among those led. The most essential work of the leader is to create more leaders."*
> –Mary Parker Follett

Creating more leaders is a force multiplier of success in your family and business. More leaders exponentially increase organizational change and innovation. More leaders equal more growth because leaders are ambitious risk takers. The more leaders your team has the more avenues, ideas and perspectives you have. Leaders lead the way to improved problem solving. The creativity and communication required for leadership provides more minds and perspectives to bring to bear on challenges.

> *"Innovation distinguishes between a leader and follower."*
> –Steve Jobs

Leadership involves intrinsic motivation and this increases the overall motivation in your team. This has an immediate positive impact on engagement, retention and every aspect of performance. Intrinsically motivated leaders also exhibit higher morale and resiliency.

We create more leaders by exhibiting leadership ourselves. When we model altruistic, vision and value-aligned leadership we inspire the leadership of others.

Have empathy for your new leaders. Consciously reflect on your first, challenging experiences leading a project or team. Imagine how much better and faster your journey of leadership would have been with the right mentor and coach. *Be that person you never had for the people you do have.* Active mentoring and coaching your people not only engages and directs their leadership development but also shows you care and creates a positive, reciprocal feedback loop.

*"Before you are a leader, success is all about growing yourself.
When you become a leader, success is all about growing others."*
–Jack Welch

Leadership is a verb more than it is a noun. Leadership is *doing* and for that to happen, people need opportunities to lead. Create that for them. Often this initial investment in developing leadership will be a loss because as you know, leadership is hard and mistakes will be made. However, people get better at the things they do consistently and your investment in your leaders will eventually break even and then be the best investment you ever made.

The leaders you make will make more leaders and the compound interest of this dynamic can change entire business and communities for generations to come. Leaders accelerate performance and create more leaders. This exponential increase in autonomy empowers performance in every aspect of your tribe.

*"A leader is best when people barely know he exists,
when his work is done, his aim fulfilled, they will say:
we did it ourselves."*
–Lao Tzu

Tribe leaders must write and speak

Where do you see your people unwilling to take leadership of projects and waiting for your decisions?

_____

_____

_____

Why do you think they are doing this? If you don't know the answer to this, *ask them.*

_____

_____

_____

Self-Relfection and Growth

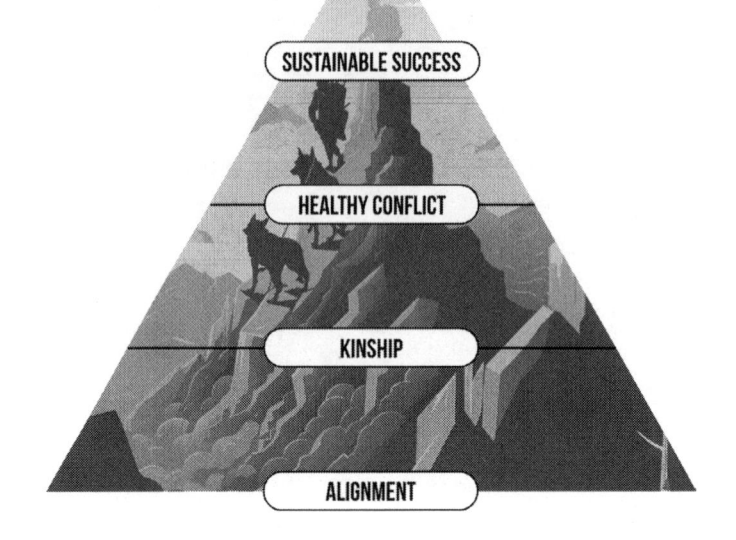

- SUSTAINABLE SUCCESS
- HEALTHY CONFLICT
- KINSHIP
- ALIGNMENT

STEP 43 UP THE TRIBE TRIANGLE:

Self-Reflection

*"If we always do what we've always done,
we will always get what we've always got."*
–Henry Ford

People have hard skills and soft skills. Hard skills are the abilities to use tools, software, data, equipment and task related proficiencies. Soft skills are the abilities to work with other people and ourselves. These soft skills include empathy, compassion, appreciation, innovation and conflict resolution.

We learn hard skills by direct feedback with our interaction with them. We learn soft skills by developing the ability to self-reflect. Self-awareness unlocks the ability to actively learn from your mistakes as well as your successes with other people and ourselves.

The time spent in self-reflection is never wasted; it is an intimate date and coaching session with yourself. Honest inventory and self-reflection opens your mind to reprogramming, change and the freedom and meaning that comes from success. It also highlights the invaluable lessons imbedded in setbacks and challenges.

The three most common learning experiences that come from self-reflection are surprise, frustration and failure. These experiences will often come from failed expectations and are where the biggest learnings exist.

Self-reflection unlocks awareness and *choice is a function of awareness.* Leadership is the study and practice of making choices that affect other people. Awareness allows us to recommit to good habits that were lost over time and empowers us to assess our strengths and failures and really see our perceptions and interactions with others.

Spending some time looking back will make the view looking forward even clearer

What are you doing and why? Are you still in alignment with your vision for the future and is it still honestly inspirational and aspirational? Are your shared values your real values that are worth the cost of all the other values that you could choose to shape your path? If you and your team are struggling to maintain success and high performance, take an honest look at those values and that vision.

> *"Your vision will become clear only when*
> *you can look into your own heart.*
> *Who looks outside, dreams; who looks inside, awakes."*
> *–Carl Jung*

Without the self-awareness that comes from self-reflection we have a massive reality blind spot that will sabotage us.

Authentic self-reflection will be a humbling experience. To discover why you feel, think, say and do what you actually do is vulnerable and revealing. It is also the most powerful leadership practice you can develop because it answers the first big question of *'Where are you'* as well as unlocking access to the last, most important question of *'who do I need to be to get there.'* Leaders who can answer these questions are the ones that sustain success over time.

We do not get strong in the gym only in recovery phase after the gym. Similarly, we only get strong in recovering from setbacks and failures in every other arena of our lives. This invaluable process of recovering from challenges is how we get stronger and more capable as leader. Self-reflection accelerates the recovery phase of growth and development.

Self-reflection over time is the process of taking an honest look at our habits and world views as well as unraveling where those beliefs and behaviors came from. If you follow that path long enough you will discover that there are some old, outdated stories and experiences from childhood that set the course you are following now. We cannot successfully navigate our path forward without looking back and in.

Like everything else in the Sustainable Success level of the Tribe Triangle, self-reflection will be connected the foundation of Alignment where the whole culture development journey started. What is your shared vision for the future and is it still the north star you are following? What are your real shared values and will they get you to that vision? Are you truly being transparent, collaborative and reciprocal in your shared missions or only when it is safe and convenient?

The process of self-reflection will enable the ability to revisit your shared vision and imagine where you really want to be in the future as well the future of your family and organization. Self-reflection also enables us to diagnose and develop our character which is the sum of our values. Self-reflection is the willingness to be with ourselves and we are too often humans who *do* as opposed to humans who are *being*.

More than anywhere else, this is where Tribe Leaders must write and speak. We are living in a time when there is very little space for self-reflection. The number one resource that industries are now clamoring for is not your money, it is your attention. Your email demands it, your phone demands it and your ever-busy life demands it. These attention demands are framed as time-sensitive priorities and the cost of reactively chasing the attention rabbit is self-awareness and reflection.

It is not enough to have an intention. If it were, we would all be in shape, rich and enlightened. Like everything else, the things that we prioritize will require the cost of all the other things that are pushed to the back burner of the life stove. This is the core of leadership.

The way we proactively make things a priority is to write them down then speak them to other people. This is how things have always been created even in mythology and religion because the power of the word is the alchemy of humanity. The universe was created with The Word and abracadabra is an ancient Hebrew word that means 'I create what I speak'. Even the word 'spelling' means both magic and writing. Recommit to writing and speaking, Tribe Leaders.

Self-reflection practices can only be made and maintained by initially carving out the time and the place you will practice your self-reflection. Like everything else, this will eventually become a habit and begin to permeate your everyday life but at first you must put this precious time on your calendar and defend it.

For many leaders, this may be one of the hardest steps up the Tribe Triangle. It is hard to spend time with ourselves without distraction. Take an honest look at any resistance you have to develop this practice this and answer these questions…

"This above all: to thine own self be true."
−William Shakespeare

Tribe leaders must write and speak

When and where will you practice your self-reflection?
___
___
___

When was the last time you experienced surprise, frustration or failure?
___
___
___

What are you spending your time doing and why?
___
___
___

Who are you spending your time with and why?
___
___
___

How are taking care of yourself and why?
___
___
___

Coaching and Standing on the Shoulders of Giants

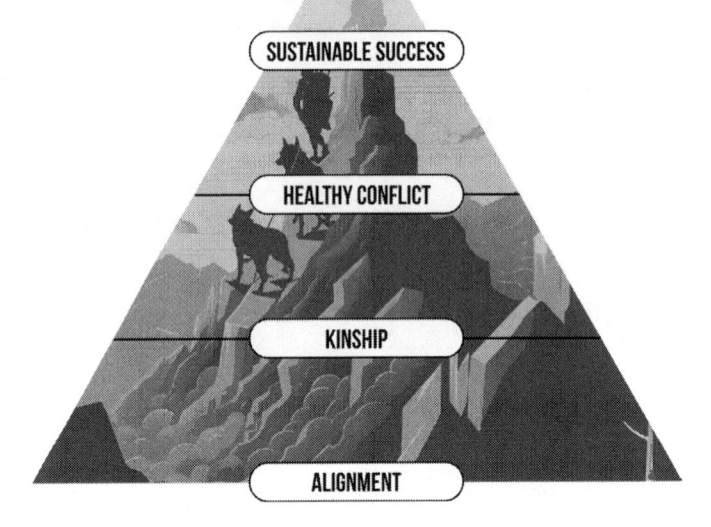

- SUSTAINABLE SUCCESS
- HEALTHY CONFLICT
- KINSHIP
- ALIGNMENT

STEP 44 UP THE TRIBE TRIANGLE:

Coaching and Standing on the Shoulders of Giants

Coaching is the universal language of leadership and learning.

If there is something in your family or team that is not as good as it could be, it is because you are not as good you could be. Getting as good as you can be, or *need* to be by yourself to achieve your goals is not only a daunting effort of trial and error but a slow one as well.

The fastest way to grow yourself is to get coached. The fastest way to grow your company is to coach your people. Coaching is the way we accelerate our people's growth and therefor our company's growth.

At the rate of change in today's constantly disruptive environment we need to maximize and accelerate our growth and development. It is no longer enough just to lead and manage our people, we need to coach them. This applies to us as well.

Coaching is cultivating your people and accelerating their evolution as both individuals and members of a community. All professional athletes have coaches and most of the highly successful professionals do too. Why not you and your team?

Coaching involves conflict which is why it can only happen effectively after the Healthy Conflict level of the Tribe Triangle. Coaching requires the illumination of our liabilities and taking people where they can't go themselves.

Coaching is about getting people to see what they *can* be instead of what they currently *are*. Coaching can and should happen at every level of the Tribe Triangle but, unfortunately, there are some associations with coaching that make people resistant to it and why it is usually only effectively implemented after the Healthy Conflict phase.

Overcoming resistance to coaching

Firstly, coaching involves conflict. You will be forced to look at your bad habits and performance issues. If you and your team have not established the Healthy Conflict phase of your culture development journey your people will not be open to coaching. Without active participation, coaching will be useless. A good coach is going to tell you and show you things that are uncomfortable to hear. That's where the growth is.

> *"A coach is someone who can give correction*
> *without causing resentment."*
> *–John Wooden.*

Secondly, coaching is a performance and success tool and until people are actually in the arena competing and both see and feel the need for coaching, there will be resistance. People will simply not accept or invest in coaching unless the fear of failure is louder than the emotional, financial and time cost.

We don't need motivation for action as much as
we need action for motivation.
Take action and find out!

Lastly, for coaching to be effective, your people need to want it and be intrinsically motivated. These people are coachable. Many are not coachable at their current state of development so invest your energy and time wisely. A good coach and mentor will both hold people accountable for their success as well as facilitate their journey toward it. We all need a fire under our asses as well as making and maintaining the fire within us.

For coaching to work, people need to want success more than the coach does. If there is resistance it will not work. People need to have the attitude and desire to be successful or coaching will never be.

Coaching is both teaching and mentoring. These two roles correspond to the hard skills and soft skills that every job or project consists of. **We teach hard skills of competence and we mentor the soft skills of character.**

In addition to teaching and mentoring, coaching is also both leadership and management which involves creating an environment so your team has every opportunity to be successful. Coaches do not just provide best practices and solutions; they ask questions. Telling people what to do solves their immediate challenges but asking questions solves their challenges in the future. This is the greatest gift you can give your people and the most significant thing you can do for both sustainable success and your legacy.

The Four Coaching Styles

There are four main categories of coaching you should be familiar with and have in your arsenal. Remember, *evolution is survival of the most adaptable* and each member of your team and each situation will require something different from you as a coach.

Direct coaching is informing people of a better way to do things. This comes from an authoritative position of skill and experience. Mentoring is an example of this coaching style. Direct coaching is immediate and targeted but does not unlock the self-directed leadership potential of your people.

The second form of coaching is *laissez-faire* which means 'hands off'. Sometimes your people may need to explore the indispensable lessons that can only come with the autonomy of direct experience. Make sure the mistakes that your people will make can be absorbed and learned from before you implement this strategy.

The third form of coaching is *non-directive*. This strategy entails a non-judgmental approach of asking questions and engaging in conversations to draw out your people's insights, feelings and thoughts about an experience or challenge. This coaching style takes longer to implement and contains less immediate results but those results are longer lasting.

Ultimately coaching is not about teaching, it is about maximizing your people's potential *to learn*.

The last and most effective of the coaching styles is *situational coaching*. This form consists of an intentional choice of *both* directive and non-directive styles based on the situation. For this strategy to be implemented effectively you will need to develop a powerful sense of empathy for the person being coached, awareness of the goal you are working toward as well as what is actually happening and the self-reflection to respond intentionally.

In many ways, you, Tribe Leader, are the head coach of your team and a team takes on the personality of its head coach. **You cannot take people past the point where you yourself have not gone.** You must be a client as well as a coach. If you are not coaching, you are allowing things to happen and at this stage of the game that trend will be away from success and down toward the level of least resistance. The Sustainable Success level of the Tribe Triangle requires that you keep your tools sharp and your people sharper.

Tribe leaders must write and speak

Where are your people struggling with maintaining success or have plateaued?

Have you established the drivers of healthy conflict that will enable coaching to be accepted and effective?

Which of the four coaching styles (Direct, Laissez-faire, Nondirective, Situational) will be most effective for your people? Is there one that you are not skillful at yet?

When was the last time *you* were coached?

Celebrations and Traditions

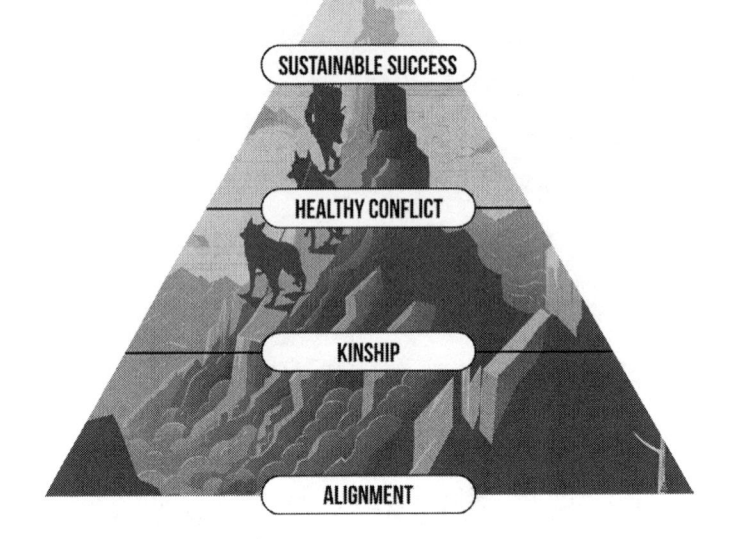

- SUSTAINABLE SUCCESS
- HEALTHY CONFLICT
- KINSHIP
- ALIGNMENT

STEP 45 UP THE TRIBE TRIANGLE:

Celebration and Traditions

"Life should not only be lived, it should be celebrated."
–Osho

The process of creating an honor-based culture in the sea of pride-based organizations is worth celebrating. It means you have not only created the most resilient and high performing team available but also reclaimed a portion of kinship for your community and our species. Kinship is what has always saved us and always will. One of the markers of kinship is shared traditions and this includes celebrations.

Traditions are the communal customs that an honor-based group participates in. They serve to hold the group together through adversity as well as success. Traditions are the glue of kinship.

The road toward your shared traditions started long ago by looking at your existing habits and the habits of your family and team. Some of these habits still serve a purpose but many are just residual behaviors that helped you to survive childhood. Most of these antiquated habits no longer serve us. If they did, you would not have gone on this journey of exploration and improvement.

Each member of your team has a unique background that generated unique survival habits and coping mechanisms. The process of exploring and upgrading these habits into more vital and successful practices is one of the greatest gifts you can give yourself and your team. An upgraded worldview and psychological operating system will carry on long after your partnerships end and ripple out into every person and organization your people interact with in the future. As leaders, we have no idea the impact our work does in the world beyond our horizon and this is worth celebrating as well. What you are doing here is important.

Remember, if there is something in you or your team's world that is not as good as it could be it is because *you and your team are not as good as you could be.*

We are a collection of our habits. To upgrade our lives we have to upgrade our habits and this demands the creation of *new practices*. As we have discussed, new practices require up to 90% more energy than habits because habits are not created for growth, they are created for efficiency. Establishing your new practices will require buy-in from your team then constant recommitment and accountability to overcome and maintain the increased energy requirements.

You can jump start this new energy system with a celebration of embarking on your journey of growth. New practices should not be framed as a punishment or other forced hardship. They should be introduced as a start of a challenging journey of success. This is a great time to revisit your inspirational shared vision for the future that anchors the journey!

You must have buy-in and excitement from your team to implement a new practice or resistance will kill it

After about a month of steady commitment to your new and demanding practices you will feel the resistance to the new load begin to fade. Many people will not notice this but you must because this is the next point of celebration. You have evolved new *rituals*.

"Remember to celebrate milestones as you prepare for the road ahead."
-Nelson Mandela

Rituals are practices that you and your team do without resistance. They are still hard but because they are now non-negotiable they are accepted and implemented regularly. You will feel and see measurable improvements with morale, engagement and all measures of sustainable success at this point.

Celebrate and appreciate yourself and your people relentlessly in this phase because this will create a ripple through your tribe as people begin to own their journey of success and actively participate at driving and sharing your new rituals.

Rituals are growth-based practices that are not only accepted but celebrated as the way we hold our standards. When these rituals are shared across the team and being organically taught to new members of the team, you have established *traditions*.

Traditions are a form of celebrations. In our current culture we have many shared traditions including holidays and sporting events. All of these traditions are celebrations or recognition and appreciation of freedom, faith, birth, death and resurrection. Simple traditions at work include putting up a picture of an employee-of-the-month or team appreciation day, company picknick or holiday parties. Even the way you kick off and close out work seasons and projects contains the potential for meaningful celebrations that weld your team together so look for opportunities to establish traditions from your new success practices. Every single chapter and theme in this book contains the potential for a tradition of celebration.

> *"The celebration of success overshadows*
> *the challenges encountered on the way."*
> *-Jeffery Benjamin*

Culture consists of shared beliefs, values and missions. Beginning that challenging shared path can be chaotic and reactive. This path will require you and your team to grow in order to be successful. To be *sustainably* successful we are going to need to implement new practices which become rituals and then traditions. Look for opportunities to recognize and celebrate every success and value-based attempt at success along the way. This is how we create meaning from all our missions, especially the hard ones.

You deserve this. Your people and projects demand it.

Tribe leaders must write and speak

You are working hard to establish new practices that improve and replace your old habits and the old habits of your team. Where is an example of these new, growth-based practices becoming established as rituals or even traditions?

_____

_____

_____

What are the ways you can celebrate these new practices and traditions? Formal and regular public acknowledgment? Formal markers of events and transitions?

_____

_____

_____

Growth Mindset and Going to War

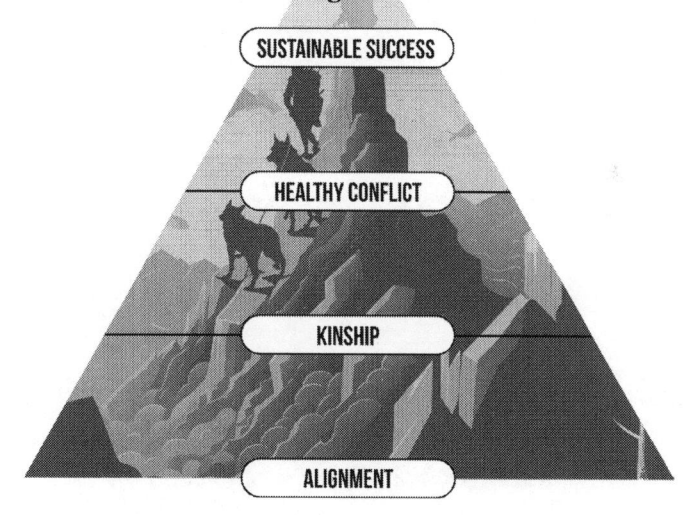

- SUSTAINABLE SUCCESS
- HEALTHY CONFLICT
- KINSHIP
- ALIGNMENT

STEP 46 UP THE TRIBE TRIANGLE:

Growth Mindset and Preparing for War

The Roman army had one of the longest runs of sustainable success in human history. To operate at this high level for so long they developed a formal, four-stage process of introducing new technology and tactics into their culture. This commitment to constant improvement and readiness for the next season of war kept their culture vital and successful for thousands of years.

The strategy of relentless improvement is known as growth mindset. It has been implemented in sports teams and other honor-based cultures throughout history and is the only antidote to the creeping death of apathy, entropy and disengagement. Chances are it will work for your family and team as well.

To implement an ongoing growth mindset, we must be able to see and acknowledge that there are cycles and seasons to all things. There are times to push hard and times to recover. Both are required for success to be sustainable. Keep this in mind as you explore the four stages of growth.

Step One, Introducing New Ideas, Technology and Tactics
"The difficulty lies not so much in developing new ideas as in escaping from the old ones."
-John Maynard Keynes

This may not appear to be the hardest step, but most families and teams get stopped at this point. **Coming up with new ideas is the easy part. Letting go of old ideas is the hard part.**

Commitment to ongoing improvement is called a growth mindset and it is a rare and hard-won component of your culture. It is so important, that most successful organizations have some version of it included in their core values. Once your people have accepted the challenges of change as normal, they will be able to bypass the initial hurdle of resistance.

Engaging in regular growth and learning represents a commitment to long-term success over short-term comfort. It takes a tremendous amount of time and energy to teach and learn something new. It also carries an additional psychological cost of frustration and humility because everything new requires a period of incompetence. This is why growth mindset can only be successfully implemented after Healthy Conflict.

> *"Every generation has underestimated the potential for new ideas. Possibilities do not add up. They multiply."*
> *-Paul Romer*

As Head of Culture, you must model this process which means you must be willing to be publicly bad at something for a period of time. This is one of the most challenging parts for leaders because we earned our leadership through competence and it is precisely this that must be modeled.

Step Two, Integration

> *"Our method was to develop integrated products, and that meant our process had to be integrated and collaborative."*
> *-Steve Jobs*

Integration is exploring and discovering where the new strategy, technology or skill fits in to your existing culture or workflow. Every change will affect both the actions leading up to the change as well as the events, decisions and actions afterwards. There is an inherent factor of stress with all change and a certain amount of stress promotes growth. Too much stress degrades performance. This is another version of Flow State that we explored in step 40.

It is important to implement changes one at a time so they don't create unmanageable chaos across your whole culture.

Finding and implementing new ideas and strategies is a skill, but integration is an art. This is the phase that your family or team will look to you for guidance. It will be hard to stay neutral and honor all sides of the conversation and process. If you are struggling with this, revisit your drivers of Kinship and Healthy Conflict because the levers of growth mindset are there. Use them.

Step Three, Hard Training

"We are what we repeatedly do. Excellence, then, is not an act but a habit."
-William Durant and Aristotle

Repetition is the mother of skill. Even when you have buy-in on your new strategy or technology and explored how it will be implemented into your workflow or culture, there is still the uphill climb toward competence. Remember, new practices take up to 90% more energy than you or your team's old habits. Also remember that it takes about 30 days to establish your new practice as a ritual. If you are lucky to have champions of change on your team you can lean on them. If not, *you may* have to be the battery that powers growth. This is what you signed up for, Tribe Leader. There are few things that will make this hard training phase easier.

Firstly, **people will only work hard at things that are worth working hard for.** Connecting these dots is your job as a leader. Have your team revisit and recommit to your shared, aspirational vision for the future. There is tremendous power locked up in hope.

"When you live for a purpose, then hard work isn't an option. It's a necessity."
-Steve Pavlina

Secondly, revisit your shared values. There should be something inherently growth or improvement oriented in these. Remind your family and team of these values as a definition of who they are. Like everything else, you will have to lead the charge on this and model the hard training required for competency.

> *"Hard work and training. There is no secret formula."*
> *-Ronnie Coleman*

Step four, Going to War

This is your time in the arena. All things have seasons even they are hard to see when you are embedded in the day-to-day grind of life. Take a good look at the big picture view of the cycles in your family and business. You will see that there are busy seasons at work, school, holidays and fitness as well as calmer times when recovery and learning must be implemented.

These seasons used to be obvious when we were more connected to the natural world. If you are involved in sports, education or other related fields, these cycles will be obvious. If not, you will have to identify and introduce these cycles to your people. We cannot be in war mode all the time and everyone needs periods of recovery after hard pushes.

Honor these cycles with your team and be intentional when your people need to recover before the introduction of the new cycle of ideas and strategies. Most importantly, honor these cycles yourself.

Tribe leaders must write and speak

When is the busy, 'going to war' season of your family or organization? When are there times for recovery and learning?

_____

_____

_____

What is an area of your family or organization that requires a new strategy, skill or system to improve or stay current?

_____

_____

_____

What is a component of your job or life that you can publicly, transparently and actively commit to growth? This will require bravery and humility because you will be modeling the struggle of improvement.

_____

_____

_____

The Strength of Vulnerability

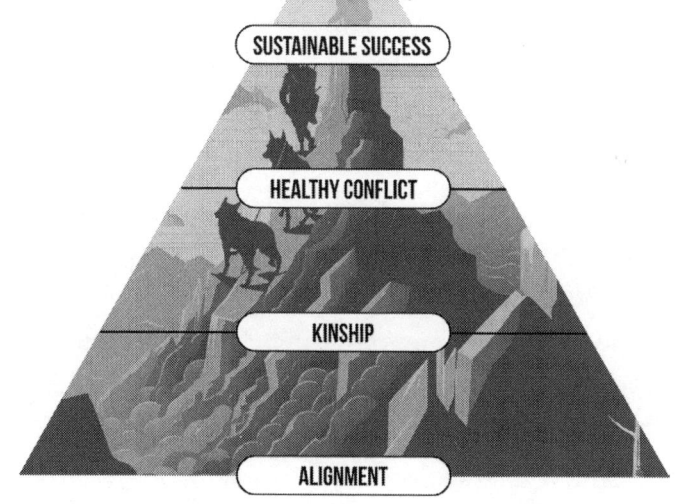

- SUSTAINABLE SUCCESS
- HEALTHY CONFLICT
- KINSHIP
- ALIGNMENT

STEP 47 UP THE TRIBE TRIANGLE:

Vulnerability

Vulnerability is a key component to sustainable success because it creates trust and reinforces strong relationships. Vulnerability is also central to the innovation and risk-taking that powers growth in every area of your family and organization. These are central pillars of maintaining high performance. Vulnerability can also be risky if not implemented skillfully and intentionally.

Vulnerability is a popular and misunderstood term these days. It is often equated with weakness and sensitivity but they are very, very different things. The difference between vulnerability and weakness is that vulnerability is a choice. It is intentionally sharing authentic challenges and feelings.

Benefits of Vulnerability

Leaders are people who make decisions that affect other people. Vulnerability is the act of intentionally choosing to be open and honest in sharing our struggles.
Intentionally choosing transparency during challenging times unlocks the potential for collaboration and reciprocity. People can only engage and support people who are open to it. This is the primary lever of creating kinship in your family and work team.

Vulnerability is also a powerful key to modeling resiliency and grit. By being honest about our experiences we unlock increased feelings of *belonging* in our relationships. Belonging creates empathy and these are the primary drivers of resiliency. You will see and feel increased connection to your people the more vulnerable you are and the challenges that would normally erode your team morale and performance will begin to augment it through the process of *trauma bonding* which is a function of vulnerability.

An additional component of resiliency is how quickly we *recover* from adversity. This is also accelerated by vulnerability. To recover from the stress of doubt and defeat efficiently we need to treat our people differently than when they are operating at their peak. We need this grace as well. Being honest and transparent with your people about your needs expedites the emotional and psychological healing process. In every spiritual practice in the world, vulnerability is central to both faith and grieving which are both core tenets of enduring and overcoming the adversities of life.

Even the ability to ask for help and delegate skillfully requires accessing vulnerability. In order to scale, grow and maintain success at high levels you will have to delegate. This means surrendering control, which for leaders is a vulnerable process because we are the ones who are ultimately responsible for the outcomes of projects.

Ultimately, true vulnerability is the ability to take risks and fail forward. It is staying in the arena when we know we can't control the outcome. It is also the ability to expose ourselves authentically to our team which is a major factor in the intimate relationships of kinship and all forms of sustainable success.

Challenges and Best Practices of Vulnerability

Vulnerability can only be implemented wisely and skillfully with the people who are not only aligned with you but also share kinship and the ability to navigate healthy conflict. These are the first three levels of the Tribe Triangle. This does not mean you can't be honest and sincere until the Sustainable Success level but too much vulnerability to soon in the wrong circles can contain blowback.

In the vast, pride-based world we all live in, vulnerability can be seen as oversharing and it often is. In the same way we must reserve our most precious resources for those special people in our kinship system, we must also reserve our most sensitive and intimate feelings for people that are safe, trustworthy and in an empathetic community. Safety, trust and empathy are all components of kinship.

In the pride-based, lone wolf world, liabilities will often be taken advantage of. There is a smart and practical level of discernment that must be implemented in these non-kinship communities. This does not imply being dishonest, or not expressing passion or ambition. It means acting appropriately based on the situation and community.

There are also times when your family and team will require you to armor up and face challenges without showing weakness. This is a valuable skill to possess but it can only be a short-term event and this is the phase of *sustainable success*. Be very mindful of this, Tribe Leader.

Vulnerability drives all forms of sustainable success including innovation, delegation and resiliency. Embracing vulnerability is another aspect of culture that you may well have to model first. It is the transition from an independent, guarded and superficial world view to the much older and more sustainably successful strategy of *interdependence*. This is tribe.

Vulnerability is a necessary component of feeling and experiencing life fully and authentically. This is the core of meaning for you and your team. It makes all the unavoidable challenges of the journey worthwhile. Vulnerability is telling the truth with courage.

Tribe leaders must write and speak

Do your family and work team express themselves with genuine vulnerability? If so, do you see it driving delegation, innovation and resiliency or is there deeper levels of vulnerability and authenticity you can model and support?

_____
_____
_____

Are there places and people that you have made the mistake of being too vulnerable and been taken advantage of? Is that experience stopping you from being vulnerable with your family and team now?

_____
_____
_____

The Holy Grail of Service

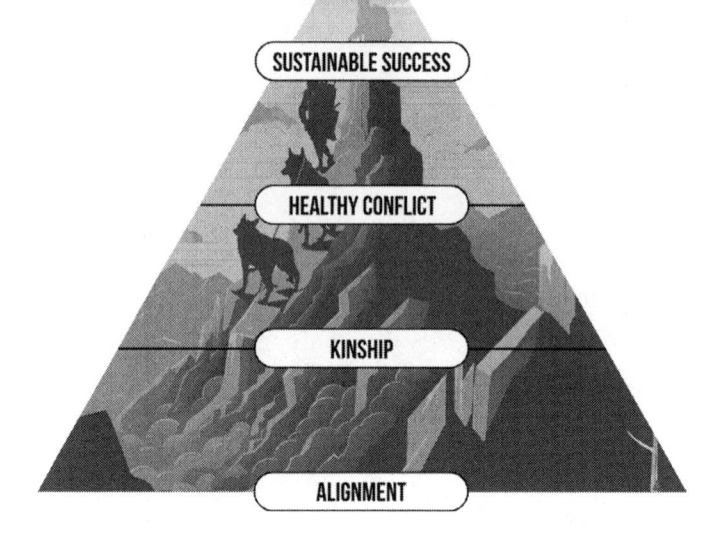

- SUSTAINABLE SUCCESS
- HEALTHY CONFLICT
- KINSHIP
- ALIGNMENT

STEP 48 UP THE TRIBE TRIANGLE:

The Power of Service

"The best way to find yourself is to lose yourself in the service of others."
–Mahatma Gandhi

Success is a noble pursuit, especially if you were unsuccessful when you were young or if you came from a family or organization with a history of personal and professional dysfunction. Becoming successful is how we initially break ancestral curses and heal ancestral wounds.

At some point that success will be revealed as a necessary but superficial accomplishment and a more worthy version of success becomes available, *sustainable success*. This more powerful impact on the world contains the development of ongoing abundance and transformation for all the people involved in your organization. Within sustainably successful families and team, leaders are born, powerful traditions are developed and the true legacy of growth across communities is established.

Embracing the components of Sustainable Success is the way we move into the service of our people and the world. This process will unlock the two big goals of life, freedom and meaning (which are covered in the next chapter).

> *"There is no higher religion than human service.*
> *To work for the common good is the greatest creed."*
> *–Woodrow Wilson*

Best Practices of Service

Service provides sustainable, meaningful engagement for your people and yourself. This important success driver comes from the fact that people will invest more and work harder for things that are significant and elevate the perceived importance of their investment of time and energy. Service sits at the top of that list of importance. There is a deep anchor of idealism and altruism to the idea of service because it is a component to all philosophies and spiritual practices throughout history. The idea of service runs deep in humanity and may well be the most important differentiator of our species.

When we believe we are providing legitimate service to people and organizations it translates to providing *value*. This is central to not only the way we do our jobs but also how we communicate what our jobs are to the world. This is an indispensable factor of marketing, brand and organizational commitment.

Very few people view selling or working for money alone favorably, however, providing value is looked at positively. Making money and serving are often the same thing and it is your job to clarify and promote the value that your people and organization is providing. If you are struggling with this, dig deeper on how and what you are doing to serve the world and how it benefits people.

In addition to how your people view providing service, your clients and community also react positively to people and organizations that are service oriented. This drives customer retention as well as community retention. Retaining friends and customers is significantly easier than finding new ones. The way you take care of people and the role you play in your community is a vital aspect of the way your personal and organizational brand is viewed in the world.

> *"People don't care how much you know until they know how much you care."*
> *-Theodore Roosevelt*

Servant leadership can be a valuable aspect of fostering the power of service in your family and organization. Servant leadership is the philosophy of supporting and championing the individuals in your team. Implementing this leadership style requires modeling the behavior of working to impower others over working for power yourself. Servant leadership is another lever in creating self-directed, intrinsically motivated people who are needed for delegating and scaling successfully. Servant leadership is a necessary component of creating other leaders.

The Challenge of Service

Ultimately sustainable service is modeled by self-care and success in the ongoing service of others. Service also must include service to self. Remember, you are the head of culture before you are anything else and if you are not acting and being sustainably successful you are not truly serving, you are being a martyr.

Service can easily slide into martyrdom if we are not building in the idea of sustainability to our schedule and workload. If you find yourself regularly putting yourself into situations where you are over-stressed and overwhelmed you have crossed into martyrdom.

Another unhealthy version of service is the inability to delegate and ask for help. This is particularly true if your reason for not reaching out is not wanting to burden others and shouldering that load yourself. Another aspect of this is making yourself constantly available and not setting healthy boundaries. We cannot continue to serve if we do not serve ourselves as well.

As leaders it is easy to slip across the unmarked line from service to martyrdom. You can see this threshold clearly by asking yourself if you are modeling the behavior that you want your team and family to emulate. Is it sustainable, vital and built on a foundation of self-interest and self-love? Remember, you are the head of culture before you are anything else and what you model is what your culture will eventually become. Your people will do what you do, not what you say, so do the right thing for yourself and the world because you are an important part of that world.

Service is not just a good way to live life, it is the way to live life *fully*. Self-interest is not selfish and service is not self-sacrifice. The martyr's message is how he sacrificed his life. The successful Tribe Leader's message is how he lived his life.

"Service to others is the rent you pay for your room here on earth."
–Muhammad Ali

Tribe leaders must write and speak

Can you crystalize the service you and your family and work team bring to the world in one sentence? If not, spend some time thinking, writing and speaking this topic to your people. It will be a valuable process and an even more valuable outcome for both you and your team.

_____

_____

_____

When does your service slide into martyrdom? Putting yourself in stressed out situations? Not asking for help? Not setting healthy boundaries?

After you have written your answer share it with your people.

_____

_____

_____

Freedom and Meaning

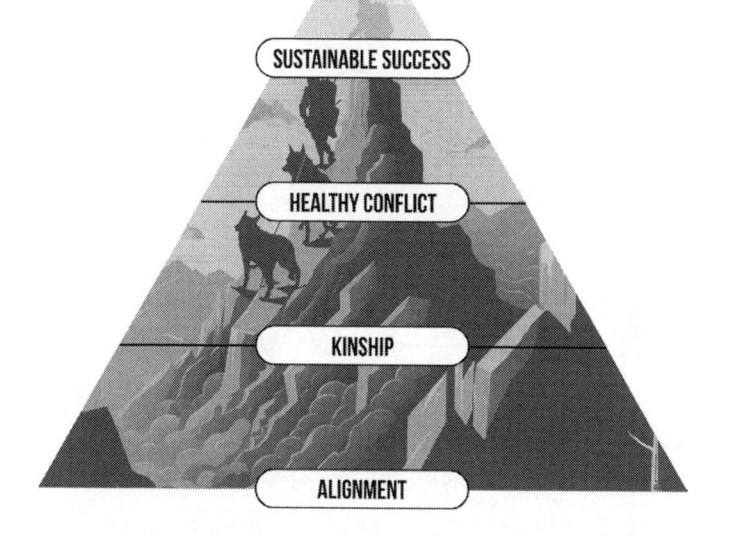

- SUSTAINABLE SUCCESS
- HEALTHY CONFLICT
- KINSHIP
- ALIGNMENT

STEP 49 UP THE TRIBE TRIANGLE:

Freedom and Meaning

"The greatest task for any person is to find meaning in his or her life."
—Victor Frankl

There is a plotline that runs through every great story of humanity. The great mythologist, Joseph Campbell, refers to it as the monomyth or the Hero's Journey. We keep retelling this great story across every generation, in every culture because it contains the unavoidable and universal sequence of human transformation but also contains the answer to what we are all truly searching for. The gold at the end of every quest is *freedom* and *meaning*. Whether you realize it or not, you are currently on your hero's journey and are the main character of the story.

Freedom

Freedom is the ability to exercise our free will; to think, speak and act how we want to and need to. It is the act of claiming our sovereignty from slavery and tyranny. This is happening in both the external and internal level of our lives and freedom in both of those worlds is interconnected. Freedom is the ability to pursue meaning.

Freedom is not just discovered and it is never given; it is won and claimed. Freedom is never free and exists on the other side of fear and sacrifice. **Freedom is never owned, it is only rented and the rent is paid in courage and discipline.** The price of freedom is due every day and often, every moment.

"Freedom, in any case, is only possible by constantly struggling for it."
-Albert Einstein

The quest for freedom takes many forms. The easiest to grapple with is financial freedom which means the ability and resources to say yes to what we want and no to what we don't. Again, this is a form of freedom that liberates us to pursue meaning which is not fully possible to commit to when we are struggling to get our basic needs met.

Freedom is the ability to have your choices be a product of your hopes and not your fears. The ability to set an aspirational vision for the future and actually commit to it is an act of true freedom and it is very rare. Now that you are aware of it, you will notice that most people are not actually in active pursuit of their dreams because they are not free enough to do it. If you are at this stage of this journey you are already aware of this and have struggled with others who lack the freedom to commit to an inspiring vision.

Often, this lack of freedom to commit to a vision for the future is not generated from an actual danger of not getting basic needs met. It is a product of a fixed mindset and a history of self-limiting beliefs. We carry these self-sabotaging mindsets with us long after they are no longer valid or practical.

Like a tourniquet, these practical priorities cut off our aspirational hopes for the future in order to survive in a challenging present. Left on too long, that self-limiting mindset tourniquet will kill the limb which must receive the blood flow of hope and meaning to survive. Playing small is easy and safe for yourself, family and team in the short-term. In the long run it is disastrous. Freedom to grow is a vital expression of self-love and the love within your culture.

> *"If you want to understand love, first understand freedom."*
> *–Paulo Coelho*

Freedom is also the ability to create. Creativity is a central part of innovation and growth of all sorts. If we do not have freedom from a fixed mindset and fear-based schedule we will prioritize survival ahead of creation. It will become something we 'get to' when we 'find the time'. Freedom unlocks this engine of expression and sustainable success.

> *"Freedom is the oxygen of the soul."*
> *–anon*

There is also the freedom from control. It is the power to say no to people and projects that are not in alignment with your family and team's shared vision and their shared values. This can be viewed as entrepreneurship, sovereignty and the freedom to make your own decisions. Freedom allows you to boldly reframe your culture in alignment with more significant, meaningful goals and behaviors.

The secret of happiness is freedom and secret of freedom is courage.

Freedom is ultimately not the right to *do as we please* (although that is part of it). True freedom is the ability and responsibility to *do what is right and important.* Freedom unlocks responsibility. Once we become free, we realize that we are now responsible for doing the right things and not the easy things.

This is where freedom connects to meaning.

Meaning

The quest for meaning is the search of why we are here and what we are and *should* be doing. This is the larger purpose of our shared vision. The vision that guides us must be significant and meaningful or it will not activate meaning within your team and will not sustain you through your ongoing quest for freedom. You do not have enough willpower or discipline to maintain growth in yourself or your team without the engine of meaning. Ultimately, our legacy will be defined by the meaningful projects and relationships that we create.

Families and organizations that have elevated their agenda from survival to meaning elevate and revitalize whole communities and industries. The ripple effect of people and teams leading meaningful lives is vast and important.

> *"The meaning of life is to live a meaningful life."*
> *−Bill Phillips*

Personal and professional meaning includes the freedom and responsibility to pursue development and transformation. It is the pursuit of our greatest potential and therefor our greatest potential to not only live and model a greater life but the ability to provide a greater service to the world. Meaning is an expression of vitality and passion. **Where our passions serve people is our purpose.**

> *"The meaning of life is to find your gift.*
> *The purpose of life is to give it away."*
> *−Pablo Picasso*

Meaning is the primary component to resiliency. If people have a strong enough *why* they can endure any *what*. Meaning is that *why*. Your shared, meaningful vision will be an important source of this meaning but the kinship level relationships will be your goldmine of meaning. If you find yourself or your team struggling with the resiliency and meaning revisit the vision and kinship components of your Tribe Triangle.

All members of your family and team are going through their own hero's journey and you also have a collective journey which is happening simultaneously. As Tribe Leader you must realize that embedded in all those quests is the pursuit of freedom and meaning. Hold that north star and be a part of that noblest human journey for your people and yourself.

Tribe leaders must write and speak

What is a self-limiting belief you see in yourself and your family or team? What is gained by claiming freedom from it? What is lost by continuing it?

_____

_____

_____

What does meaning mean to you within your family and team? Is it personal development and reaching full potential? Is it service to each other and the world? This is an invaluable conversation to have with your people at this point in the journey and will unlock increased sustainable success.

_____

_____

_____

Becoming a Professional

- SUSTAINABLE SUCCESS
- HEALTHY CONFLICT
- KINSHIP
- ALIGNMENT

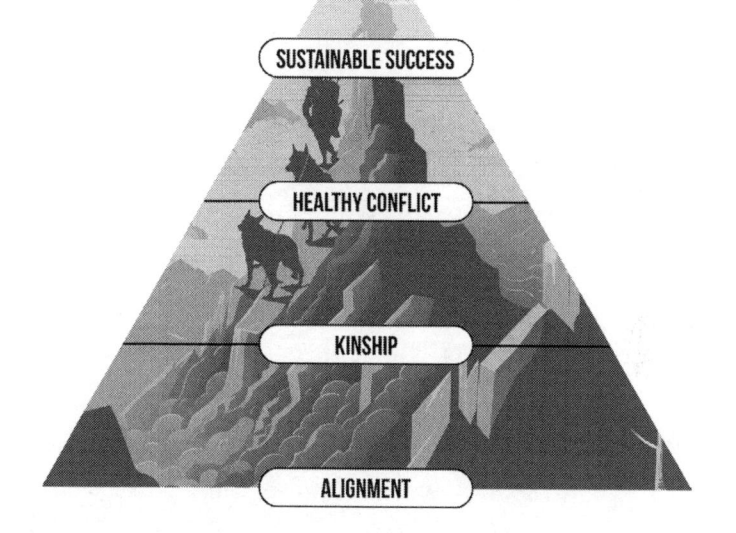

STEP 50 UP THE TRIBE TRIANGLE:

Becoming a Professional

"A professional is someone who can do his best work when he doesn't feel like it."
—Alistair Cooke

Being a professional does not mean just getting paid or having achieved a certain level of skill although it does eventually include both of those valuable things. Being a professional is at its core, a mindset and an identity that is central to sustainable success. Being a professional is a way of doing things long before it is a result.

Being a professional at something means it is your priority. It is a central aspect to what you do every day. A professional is not defined by what they do *occasionally*, that is a hobbyist. A professional is defined by what we do *consistently*. Developing consistency is the way we intentionally do things that are directed at an intentional outcome. It is the birth of professionalism.

Consistency is the foundation of success in every arena. People who do things consistently and intentionally become successful at that thing. Eventually this process does lead to the high levels of skill and money that are commonly connected to being a professional but the consistency comes first. Long before anyone is viewed as a professional, they were practicing it. This requires an elevated and profound sense of self and our destiny.

"The question isn't who is going to let me; it's who is going to stop me."
-Ayn Rand

Developing the habits that define professionalism is a demanding journey but you have already explored many of these concepts in your tribe development journey. They are all well worth revisiting and recommitting to at this stage of Sustainable Success. This may be one of the most important behaviors that you will need to model as Head of Culture. As you explore the best practices of professionalism make sure you are looking at how you are currently implementing them and where you can install some upgrades.

Professionals operate by a set of values

Being a professional means living by a professional ethos. This code guides our behavior which means it guides our decisions and actions. As we meet the 6000 significant choices we are faced with every day, make sure that the way you are responding to them is not reactive. We must follow the north star of our professional values if we are to live and act like professionals.

Professionals do the values-driven work. Not when they are *inspired or have the time or feel like it.* We do the important work because the work is us. **We understand that work is not a product of inspiration, inspiration is a product of the work.**

> *"The professional does not wait for inspiration;*
> *he acts in anticipation of it."*
> *–Steven Pressfield*

Professionals follow a vision for the future

Being a professional is not only having a clear vision for the future but intentionally and relentlessly working toward it. The unspoken part of this journey toward a future that is inspiring and aspirational is the sacrifice of all the other competing visions for the future. This involves focus, and remember, focus is *subtractive.* It means saying no to all the other choices and dreams that are constantly competing for our attention, time and energy.

The professional journey toward our vision involves the continual setting and recommitment of goals. This is an indispensable part of professionalism. Model this and instill this as part of you and your team's ethos. For professionals, opportunities don't happen, we create them.

> *"Setting goals is the first step in turning the invisible into the visible."*
> *—Tony Robbins*

Professionals are willing to sacrifice

Following a code of values and relentlessly recommitting to a vision is hard. The life of the professional and the amateur are both hard but the challenges of the profession contain meaning, hope and energy that makes all the difference. We must learn to love the professional sacrifice of discipline and *embrace the suck*.

We all fail. Amateurs who fail accept it as who they are or more commonly, process failure by blaming someone or something outside themselves. Professionals take responsibility for the failure and respond to it as a painful but valuable learning experience.

> *"If you can't fly then run, if you can't run then walk,*
> *if you can't walk then crawl, but whatever*
> *you do you have to keep moving forward."*
> *Martin Luther King*

The professional is always committed to the sacrifice of learning. This means they are always willing to be bad at things. Professionals know that at some point they will become good and *then* great. Understand the magnitude, cost and impact of this cycle deeply because you will usually not want to be doing it. In fact, most of the professional life consists of things you may not *want* to be doing but *need* to be doing. **The burden of the professional is that good must be sacrificed for great.** This requires resiliency. Be very mindful of this for yourself, your family and your team. Stay positive during this process. Being positive in negative situations is not naïve, it's a professional leadership survival skill.

Professionals realize that the learning process from bad to good to great is unavoidable and ongoing. They also know that they cannot do this alone. All professionals carve out and defend the time to practice being bad so they can work at being great. They also know that they need outside accountability to sustain this process and accelerate it with coaching. All professionals practice and all have coaches. Reflect deeply on this.

Professionals are always looking for improvement and growth. This is a central component to living a life of meaning. It also carries a heavy burden of discipline and the knowledge that you will never truly arrive at your destination of mastery. The journey toward that goal contains the same number of challenges as the journey of the amateur but the challenges are vastly more inspiring, meaningful and rewarding. You deserve it. Your people and projects demand it.

> *"The only way to do great work is to love what you do. If you haven't found it yet, keep looking. Don't settle."*
> *–Steve Jobs*

Tribe leaders must write and speak

What is a primary competency that you recognize you need to develop to a professional level? What are the new behaviors you must implement to achieve this? How are they reflected in your ethos and values and do those need to be revisited?

_____

_____

_____

Have you and your family and team carved out time in your schedule to practice the process of being bad at a skill so it can become good and then great? Do you have a coach?

_____

_____

_____

Recommit and Reconnect

- SUSTAINABLE SUCCESS
- HEALTHY CONFLICT
- KINSHIP
- ALIGNMENT

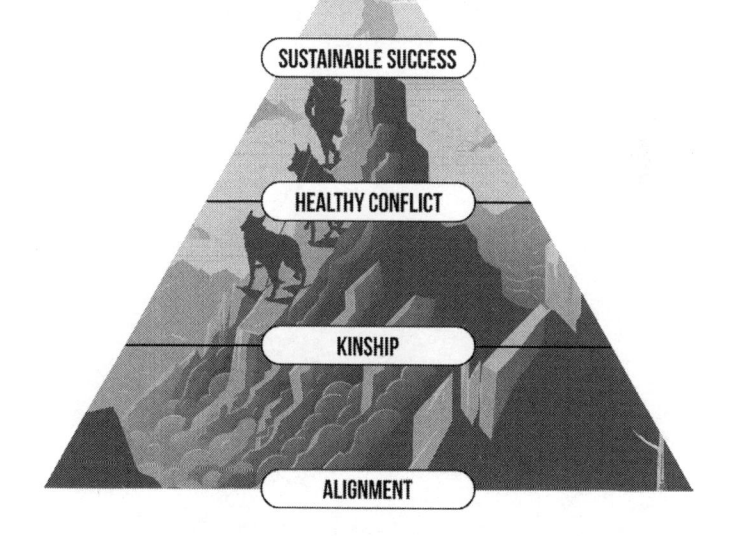

STEP 51 UP THE TRIBE TRIANGLE:

Recommit and Reconnect

Very simply, individual and group success requires commitment and connection. *Sustainable* success requires *recommitment* and *reconnection*. As leaders we must be aware when these core requirements within ourselves and our team show up and we need to respond decisively and skillfully when they do.

The foundation of sustainable success for your family and organization was built on a shared vision for the future, a shared set of values that gets you there and shared missions that are transparent, collaborative and reciprocal. All of that led to kinship and all the power and resiliency of those robust relationships. It is a very common mistake of leadership to think that once the alignment work and kinship work is done that its *actually* done. This is never the case. Like every other system in the world, that foundation will tend toward entropy and will need revitalization.

Recommitment

*"Motivation is what gets you started.
Commitment is what keeps you going."
-Jim Rohn*

For athletes and other professionals, recommitment is an accepted part of the success process and is built into their life strategy. They know that things are going to knock them and their team off course and that setbacks happen. These challenges may include the loss of a valuable team member, addition of a new team member, changes in their industry or unavoidable personal challenges such as loss or injury. Even boredom and burnout are normalized as an accepted part of their journey and actively addressed with recommitment. That is the nature of life and the pursuit of success.

Each one of these setbacks is a form of stress and trauma. Some will be small inconveniences and some will be major events that force us to reexamine our foundation of alignment and how well our kinship system is working. This does not invalidate your foundation of shared vision you are working toward or your shared values. It simply means you facing a challenge. **More often than not, struggles will be a lesson on the need to recommit to those things, not abandon them.**

Recommitment is a skill like any other and it will get better with time. Understanding the need for recommitment and both how and when to utilize it is a primary driver of sustainable success in all the relationships and practices of your life. Your primary tool for dealing with these challenges is the kinship function of resiliency and recommitment is a primary function and driver of resiliency. Even resiliency practices themselves require regular recommitment or they will slip into disuse.

You cannot have ongoing commitment without recommitment. The commitments we have to our vision, organization and each other are only as strong as our ability to recommit. We are living in the *attention age* and there have never been more forces clamoring for our focus and resources. Recommitment to our larger purpose in the world is the strategy to combat these distractions. Your team may be resistant to regular recommitment but simply talking about them is revitalizing and one of your central functions as Head of Culture.

May is National Recommitment Month which is an opportunity for leaders and organizations to reflect on their vision, values and goals with the collective support of large numbers of people across the country. This is a chance to sharpen your saw and regain your focus on the significant, purposeful direction you are heading. I propose that every month be recommitment month with additional recommitment enacted after every major success and particularly, after every failure.

Reconnection

FEAR can mean Forget Everything and Run
or it can mean Find Everything and Reconnect."
–Sanjay Patel

People change. You want them to and this is an important part of the culture development journey. Your culture is the behavior of your people and for your culture to change and grow your people must also. As you and your people transform, paths will begin to diverge. Some people will need new challenges and responsibilities to match their new sills. Some of your people will require more peace and control to match their new priorities. To keep diverging paths connected you will need to reconnect.

As your people grow, they will begin to find new levels of authenticity in how they express themselves and how they need to be communicated with. Almost all disagreements and relationship fractures come from a failure to communicate clearly and skillfully. Misunderstandings are the source of almost all conflict. It is worth revisiting the communication styles chapter in this book when you see inevitable conflicts appear in your family and team.

We are changing too. Leadership changes us and so will every decision, action, defeat and victory we experience. It will be impossible to have not changed if you have done even a few of the Tribe Leader writing challenges. When we reconnect with our tribe we reconnect to ourselves.

People will come and people will go. This is a natural and unavoidable part of being part of a team. Reconnection is vital for managing the addition or departure of people from your tribe. Successful onboarding of new people and taking care of people after the exit of others is vital for maintaining kinship in your family and team. Have any arrival or departure of people be an automatic trigger for a reconnection ritual.

Kinship is an intimate thing. Many people have not experienced it since their time in the military or team sports as a youth. Many have never experienced kinship and it can be both a euphoric and overwhelming thing. For some of those people, it will be an easy backslide into shallowness or even isolation. Reconnection is the maintenance work to keep the engine of kinship running and producing results. Revisit and reflect on what reconnection traditions such as celebrations and public acknowledgments you have established in your culture. Even modeling the transparency of asking for help and appreciations are simple but profound acts of reconnection.

> *"All things are connected like the blood that unites us.*
> *We do not weave the web of life, we are merely a strand in it.*
> *Whatever we do to the web, we do to ourselves."*
> *–Chief Seattle*

Recommitment and reconnection are an endless process and it can feel like the Greek character Sisyphus endlessly pushing his rock uphill only to see it roll back down after all his effort. The stoics interpreted that story not as a punishment but as an example of a life of profound meaning and noble struggle. The sun must rise again every day without complaint and this is what you signed up for, Tribe Leader.

Tribe leaders must write and speak

Where are you seeing or feeling symptoms of disengagement or burnout in yourself, family or team? What important thing do you need to recommit to? Your aspirational vision for the future? Guiding values that get you there? The meaningful shared missions you are working on? Your team needs to hear this as much as you do.

_____

_____

_____

Where are you seeing or feeling symptoms of conflict or distance with your family or team? Have you or your people changed and need to be reconnected and appreciated? Are there communication tools that need to be sharpened to resolve and avoid conflict? Does your team need a celebration tradition to reopen the flow of vitality and kinship?

_____

_____

_____

The Legacy of Recliming Kinship

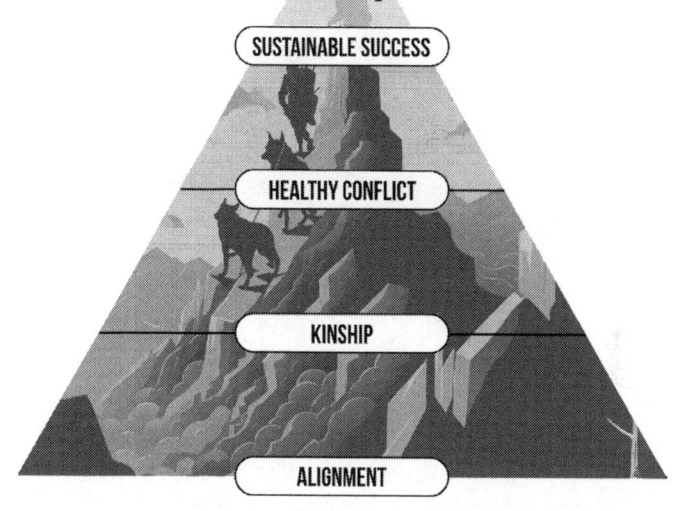

- SUSTAINABLE SUCCESS
- HEALTHY CONFLICT
- KINSHIP
- ALIGNMENT

STEP 52 UP THE TRIBE TRIANGLE:

The Legacy of Reclaiming Kinship

"It is not the level of prosperity that makes for happiness, but the kinship of heart to heart and the way we look at the world."
–Alexander Solzhenitsyn

Alignment and kinship are the base of the Tribe Triangle as well as the foundation of both culture and humanity itself. Alignment and kinship are the two components of an honor-based culture which has evolved over hundreds of thousands of years to meet the survival needs of humans and give us a chance to thrive in a challenging world. The world that generated the honor-based culture of tribe also reinforced and rejuvenated it with regular and repeated real-life lessons. These lessons are now hidden from us by the success of our species. Like the fall of all great empires, our success contains the seeds of our undoing.

As we developed industrial farming that removed the need to hunt and grow our own food, invented climate-controlled living environments and removed all forms of predation, we also lost the drivers of alignment and kinship. Meaningful connections with the people we live and work with has become a seemingly optional investment.

> *"Humans become human through intense learning not just of survival skills but of customs and social mores, kinship and social laws–that is, culture."*
> *- Richard Leakey*

Our current pride-based, me-centric world is proving to be disastrous for the physical, mental and emotional health of humanity. Stress-related illness and death are rising. So are clinical anxiety, depression, addiction and suicide that are now at epidemic rates. Feelings of loneliness and isolation are now accepted as normal. None of this is natural and none are healthy.

The solution to these critical challenges is to keep and celebrate the food, shelter and safety advances of our society while reintroducing kinship back into our close communities that require it. The work you are doing on these 52 steps is reclaiming our birthright of kinship.

> *"The first lesson of evolution was one of conflict.*
> *The lesson now is one of kinship."*
> *- Holmes Rolston III*

We will never go back to the time of tribes and villages and that is a good thing. Our destiny is at the scope and scale of the stars. While we cannot create kinship within groups as large as cities and nations, we can and must own the small cultures in which we spend most of our time. This is our immediate family and community and the team or department we work in. This hybrid model of humanity provides the health, meaning and belonging that can only come from kinship while still maintaining the pursuit of our unique destiny as a conscious species.

The kinship work you are doing with your family and work team is transforming the world. It may be the most legacy-producing labor in your entire life. When people experience the belonging of tribe they heal mentally, emotionally and physically. They become more functional at home and at work. This increased vitality directly impacts everyone they interact with at school, in their communities and with coworkers and clients. The ripple effect of healthy humanity has a vastly broader influence than we can ever imagine.

> *"The influence of vital people vitalizes."*
> *-Joseph Campbell*

Like everything else on this epic journey up the Tribe Triangle this process begins with you, Tribe Leader. Whether you have started this project as the pursuit of personal family and career improvement or answering the call to understand and solve some of the big challenges that are facing society today, all roads lead to kinship and belonging.

Remember Ubuntu, *I am because we are and we are because I am.* You are an indispensable component to your family and team. You *are* them and they *are* you. You are not sacrificing yourself for your people; you are celebrating yourself. There is no greater expression of love for yourself than to have your people growing and thriving.

> *"Kinship: not serving the other but being one with the other."*
> *-Greg Boyle*

We are currently facing new challenges at a scale and pace never experienced by humanity. Many of these challenges are at an international and global scale. Most of us simply do not have the operating system, position or resources to engage with many of the trials of this magnitude.

We do however, have the operating system, position and resources to address those challenges with the people and projects that we interact with every day. We may not be able to save the world but we can save our partners, our families, our communities and our work team. As leaders, creating the powerful social cohesion of kinship is our responsibility and our duty. You now have the map and it is your challenge to use it and answer the call to the create kinship. It has always saved us and it always will. Think globally. Act locally.

> *"A community is made up of intimate relationships among diversified types of individuals-a kinship group, a local group, a neighborhood group, a village, a large family."*
> *-Carroll Quigley*

Tribe leaders must write and speak

When you reflect on the beginning of your journey up the Tribe Triangle it started with the establishment of an aspirational vision to share with your family and team. What are some measurable successes in your family and team? What is the future impact of this vision on the rest of the world?

_____

_____

_____

"Whatever you are doing, take the attitude of wanting it directly or indirectly to benefit others. Take the attitude of wanting it to increase your experience of kinship with your fellow beings." – Pema Chodron

Common leadership and culture challenges and the Tribe Triangle step solutions

The Tribe Triangle is your roadmap for creating a resilient and sustainably high performing team from a collection of individuals.

It can also be used a diagnostic tool to find solutions to the most common and pressing challenges in your family and work team. Below you will find a list of some of these challenges and the chapters that will provide information and solutions.

Low Engagement
- Step 3 31
- Step 4 36
- Step 7 56
- Step 23 148
- Step 41 249
- Step 42 255
- Step 48 290
- Step 49 295

Low Retention
- Step 4 36
- Step 6 49
- Step 7 56
- Step 23 148
- Step 25 161
- Step 32 197
- Step 43 262

Low Morale
- Step 10 75
- Step 11 81
- Step 17 119

- Step 23 148
- Step 25 161
- Step 31 192
- Step 36 219
- Step 45 274

Communication Challenges
- Step 4 36
- Step 8 62
- Step 19 129
- Step 20 133
- Step 24 154
- Step 31 192
- Step 34 207
- Step 47 285

Burn Out and Low Resiliency
- Step 4 36
- Step 6 49
- Step 16 114
- Step 18 124
- Step 35 214
- Step 39 235
- Step 41 249
- Step 47 285

Lack of Accountability
- Step 6 49
- Step 8 62
- Step 12 87
- Step 13 93
- Step 27 171
- Step 28 176

- Step 34 207
- Step 42 255
- Step 50 301

Lack of Innovation
- Step 12 87
- Step 19 129
- Step 29 182
- Step 30 187
- Step 32 197
- Step 38 230

Lack of Motivation and Initiative
- Step 4 36
- Step 6 49
- Step 7 56
- Step 16 114
- Step 21 138
- Step 23 148
- Step 25 161
- Step 26 165
- Step 33 202
- Step 42 255
- Step 48 290

An Ancient Blessing for Modern Tribe Leaders and an Invitation

"If you are not for yourself, who will be?
If you are not for others, what are you?
If not now, when?"
-Rabbi Hillel the Elder

If you are not for yourself, who will be?

Ubuntu means we are because I am. You are as important and vital as any member of your tribe. Live like it. If you are not championing yourself and your unique and aspirational vision for the future who will be? You must care about your vision and your legacy more than anyone else. This means moving without permission and without any guarantees.

Being for yourself also includes self-care. You are the Head of Culture before you are anything else and if you are not practicing your own resiliency, forgiveness and grace you cannot expect your team to model this. It is your responsibility to practice and recommit to sustainable success.

If you are not for others, what are you?

Live your life in service and be compensated for it in every way. Ubuntu means I am because we are. Your shared vision, values and mission must include everyone. Your tribe defines you as does all your group projects.

Nothing significant can be done alone. There must collaboration, delegation and all other forms of pack hunting to bring down the big game of meaning and legacy. Your vision depends on it. This is the backbone of all forms of sustainable success. The journey up the Tribe Triangle is more than just the creation of sustainable success for your family and organization. It also is the process of humanity reclaiming our birthright of kinship. Without this vital form of reciprocal honor and resiliency we will continue to collapse into loneliness, anxiety, depression, addiction and suicide.

If not now, when?

We are living in artificial times where the natural world is no longer shoving us with her powerful hands. We are never hungry, cold or hunted. Kinship is seen as an optional experience instead of a survival strategy. It is easy to wait for 'when we're ready' or 'when we get the time'. Often, we are waiting for some form of permission from authority to start. You, Tribe Leader, are the source of your own permission and your people are waiting on you.

In this book we have explored how to implement the ancient African success philosophy, Ubuntu *(I am because we are and we are because I am)* into our modern family and work team. An even older version of this statement is the law of the wolves framed by Rudyard Kipling: *The strength of the pack is the wolf and the strength of the wolf is the pack.*

Far beyond the history of humanity, the wolves ran this operating system for millions of years with tremendous success. A lone wolf has a short lifespan of scavenging and hunting unsubstantial, small prey. A wolf pack at full power is the apex predator of its ecosystem and capable of hunting the largest animals on the planet. The wolves lived Ubuntu long before we did and were the source of this success philosophy for us.

300,000 years ago, during the era of domination by the wolves a strange new species evolved in the savannahs of Africa; *us*. For most of our history we were an unsuccessful species scavenging the leftovers of successful predators. We were able to crack open long bones for marrow with primitive stone tools and survive the night huddled around our fires. Even with our new, larger brains we invented nothing and the making of our stone tools and use of fire were skills passed on by long-extinct ancestors. For much of our existence homo sapiens' numbers were so low we were below the extinction threshold. By all measures we were an unsuccessful species.

We migrated up into Europe around 40,000 years ago with our meagre numbers and primitive skills and there we met an even greater challenge, neandertals and the wolves. Both of these competitive species were long adapted to the climate and the skills to survive there. The neandertals were larger, stronger, had larger brains and used the same tool kit as we did. We had little chance to compete against this established, cold-adapted species. Things were bleak indeed for our brave ancestors.

Something magical happened 35,000 years ago that transformed the path of our unsuccessful, scavenger ancestors and the entire world; we managed to partner with the apex predator on planet earth, the wolf. This alliance and what we gained from it triggered a sudden and complete transformation of our species. From this one clear point in the timeline of human history we see the explosion of modern culture including complex ritual burials, symbolic thought, musical instruments, carved game pieces, advanced hunting technology and most importantly the ability to not just scavenge the leftovers of big game but successfully bring it down.

We did not domesticate the wolf. The wolf domesticated us.

What were the secrets we learned from the established apex super predator, the wolf? What were the lessons that enabled our immediate and profound cultural transformation? To understand this, we must take a deep dive into what made the wolf the most successful, adaptable communal hunter on the planet and how that lupine tool kit made us the most successful species on earth.

Please take this journey with me into the wisdom of the wolves and how it transformed us from a state of surviving to thriving. The lessons still work today and are more in need now than any time in recent history. Philipfolsom.com

Ubuntu,
Philip Folsom

Made in the USA
Monee, IL
16 October 2024